Cooperative Work Groups

This book is dedicated to Aaron Moretzsky, one of the finest educators I have ever known. Before his retirement this past year as Assistant Principal at Pacoima Middle School in Los Angeles, Aaron was the heart and soul of our school. His leadership, guidance, friendship, and awesome editing abilities made me a better teacher, writer, and person over the past ten years.

Cooperative Work Groups

Preparing Students for the Real World

Scott M. Mandel

CORWIN PRESS, INC.
A Sage Publications Company
Thousand Oaks, California

For information:

Corwin Press, Inc.
A Sage Publications Company
2455 Teller Road
Thousand Oaks, California 91320
www.corwinpress.com

Sage Publications Ltd.
6 Bonhill Street
London EC2A 4PU
United Kingdom

Sage Publications India Pvt. Ltd.
B-42, Panchsheel Enclave
Post Box 4109
New Delhi 110 017 India

Printed in the United States of America

Library of Congress Cataloging-in-Publication Data

Mandel, Scott M.
Cooperative work groups: Preparing students for the real world / Scott M. Mandel.
    p. cm.
Includes bibliographical references and index.
ISBN 0-7619-3876-1 (Cloth) — ISBN 0-7619-3877-X (Paper)
    1. Group work in education. 2. Team learning approach in education.
3. Multiple intelligences. 4. Internet in education. I. Title.
LB1032.M364 2003
371.39´5—dc21

2003005946

03   04   05   06   10   9   8   7   6   5   4   3   2   1

Acquisitions Editor:	Kylee M. Liegl
Editorial Assistant:	Jaime L. Cuvier
Production Editor:	Melanie Birdsall
Copy Editor:	Kristin Bergstad
Typesetter:	C&M Digitals (P) Ltd.
Proofreader:	Tricia Toney
Indexer:	Michael Ferreira
Cover Designer:	Michael Dubowe
Production Artist:	Lisa Miller

Contents

Acknowledgments

This book could not have been produced without the tremendous help of a number of very talented people. First and foremost, I want to thank my editor at Corwin Press, Kylee Liegl, for her wonderful support and assistance throughout the process. Also at Corwin, I want to thank Editorial Assistant Jaime L. Cuvier, Production Editor Melanie Birdsall, Copyeditor Kristin Bergstad, and C&M Digitals (P) Ltd.

A number of educators in the Los Angeles Unified School District lent their hand to this work. I owe a tremendous amount of gratitude to Aaron Moretzsky for his invaluable editing on the original manuscript. I want to thank Melodie Bitter and Robert Schuck for their input and feedback in the development of this book.

Finally, I want to thank Don Sostarich and the folks at Pearson Professional Development in Chicago who allowed me to develop and teach summer teacher education courses on Cooperative Work Groups, enabling me to test and refine the concepts and material found in this book.

Corwin Press gratefully acknowledges the contributions of the following reviewers:

Lynne Beachner
St. Francis Xavier School
Kansas City, MO

Carole Biskar
Tualatin Elementary School
Tualatin, OR

Richard J. Marchesani
Elmira College
Elmira, NY

Anola Pickett
St. Francis Xavier School
Kansas City, MO

About the Author

 **Scott M. Mandel** received his Ph.D. in Curriculum and Instruction from the University of Southern California. A National Board Certified teacher, he still remains in the classroom in the Los Angeles Unified School District. The author of nine teacher education books, Mandel is also the Founder and Director of the Teachers Helping Teachers Web site: www.pacificnet.net/~mandel.

Introduction

WHY COOPERATIVE WORK GROUPS?

A Story: Designing an Ecosystem

Ms. Johnson was developing her "ecosystems" curriculum for her science class. As a means of synthesizing the material and concepts at the end of the unit, she developed a project where her students would create their own ecosystem. She decided that a cooperative work group experience would be the most successful and efficient way of implementing this design.

At the beginning of the project, Ms. Johnson gave the following scenario to her class:

"The world is rapidly becoming overpopulated, and adequate living space is becoming increasingly scarce. You do not want to have rain forests cleared for human habitation, because of the negative consequences to the environment. Living under the oceans is not feasible, because the technology does not yet exist for this to occur. Therefore, we are going to determine whether or not humans can create a self-sufficient area on land that is underutilized, and that would not negatively impact the global environment.

"You will create a self-sufficient ecosystem in the desert of the Southwest United States. The civilization you create should address all of the necessities of human life, so as to be self-sufficient without any need for physical contact with the outside world."

Ms. Johnson then provided the students with an actual map of approximately one hundred square miles of uninhabited desert in the American Southwest, ensuring that the selected area did have some farmable land and water available.

As the first step, the class worked as a unit to discuss how to approach their project. They determined that they would break into six different research groups to study material in their area and then report back to the class as a whole. The students decided on the basic direction of each of the individual groups. Ms. Johnson then assigned students to each of the groups, based on her knowledge of the students, and the requirements of the proposed group tasks.

The following is a description of the six groups, significant factors in their organization, and a brief summary of their basic research and work:

Culture: The Arts

The class determined that every civilization had a particular culture, and that their new environment required the same. This group specially included some students with a high multiple intelligence in the spatial, bodily-kinesthetic, and musical areas. Using the Educational Resources page of the general education

Internet site, TEACHERS HELPING TEACHERS,[1] they investigated the cultures of the American Southwest, including Native American, Hispanic, and Western culture. Using this information, they created some original music, art, and drama, integrating the material they developed with their own cultures.

Culture: Everyday Life

Other aspects of everyday culture—besides food and clothing—were integrated into this group's research. This consisted of aspects of everyday life including the life of children, and areas of recreation not covered by the other culture groups. The students used the Internet sites researched by the "Culture: The Arts" group, in addition to literature concerning life in this area over the past few hundred years. The heavy literature component required that this group include students with a high linguistic multiple intelligence.

Geography

The primary responsibility of this group was determining exactly where to construct their "community." The students focused their investigation on the physical features of the land, available water resources, and climatic variations in the region. The group deliberately included students with high logical-mathematical and naturalist multiple intelligences. For data, they closely studied the area, incorporating maps that they located on the Internet. They also incorporated a number of online sites found on the general education site, TEACHERS HELPING TEACHERS.

People of the Region

This group investigated the lifestyles of people who had inhabited this region. They concentrated on how humans adapted to this particular environment, including types of clothing worn, and food grown and consumed. They incorporated material from the general education Internet site cited above, as well as usable material at specialized Internet sites such as DESERT LIFE IN THE AMERICAN SOUTHWEST.

Shelter

These students studied the cultures investigated in the "People of the Region" group, in addition to other unique adaptations humans made to survive in extreme climates, by using a number of the Internet sites incorporated by the other groups. The group specifically included students with a high spatial multiple intelligence, for they analyzed and synthesized the material that they discovered to design buildings and living areas for their "community" that would be efficient and adaptable to an extreme and harsh climate.

Wildlife/Food

This group investigated the multifarious types of animals and plants of the region, to determine which could be used as food sources. Furthermore, they also studied the role played by the various forms of wildlife within the desert ecosystem, so as not to disrupt the ecosystem. The students used numerous Web sites incorporated by the other groups, plus a number of science-related sites located on TEACHERS HELPING

TEACHERS. Students with a high naturalist multiple intelligence were especially included in this group.

The final result of this extended cooperative work group project was a self-sufficient prototype community in the Southwestern United States desert that synthesized the various ideas and information accrued by Ms. Johnson's students throughout their unit on ecosystems.

THE NEW CLASSROOM BATTLE: WHAT TODAY'S BUSINESSES WANT VERSUS TRADITIONAL TEACHING

Although not very "research based," popular sentiment of "life in corporate America today" is demonstrated in a comic strip called Dilbert (©United Feature Syndicate, Inc.). The feature regularly includes a number of employees (engineers) in cubicles, working on tasks. A central theme of the comic strip involves the individuals coming together and working as a unit on a common project—in other words, they are required to function as a cooperative work group.

Individuals working together in groups on long-term projects are fundamental in today's work society. The situation is also diametrically opposite to the way students are usually taught. The primary mode of instruction in K-12 educational institutions around the country is still overwhelmingly frontal teaching by the instructor (or through a lesson presented in a passive text book), followed by individual practice of the curricular material.

Whereas these teaching methodologies may prepare the students with the specialized curricular knowledge necessary to succeed on standardized testing, unfortunately they do not ready students for successful employment in the twenty-first century. No longer is the individual seen as a "cog in the system," as portrayed in the Scientific Management school of thought.[2]

Today's businesses want workers who can function both independently and within groups, who can successfully and productively collaborate with coworkers on projects, and who can view themselves holistically within the overall organization (see Carnevale, 1991, 1996, 2002; Carnevale, Gainer, & Meltzer, 1990; Carnevale & Porro, 1994). In addition, in the past decade there has been a growing trend toward worker participation in management. Such units within the business world are commonly referred to as self-managing teams, self-directed work groups, quality circles, autonomous work groups, or cross-functional teams, and reflect this move toward collaborative-styles of management (Jacobs & James, 1994; Kozlowski, 1995).

Businesses have become increasingly aware of the inability of workers to function in this type of cooperative environment. In turn, business schools have been pressured to emphasize in their programs the communication processes necessary for success in this type of corporate setting, and to provide their students with experiences in which they can practice these critical skills (Wayne et al., 1992; see also Barker, Gilbreath, & Stone, 1998). It follows that a logical place to start teaching these basic interpersonal work skills is in the K-12 educational system.

Unfortunately, cooperative working skills are not included on standardized tests, and are not emphasized, or even mentioned, in local or state educational standards. In today's political climate, where the value and success of the educational process is directly linked to publishable test scores, cooperative work experiences are either de-emphasized or ignored. This creates a learning environment that is diametrically opposite to that which is required in the work world.

It is critical for teachers to ensure that their students are prepared for the challenges of the twenty-first century workplace. The emphasis on standardized testing results is not expected to diminish any time soon—especially with the tremendous emphasis on test results espoused by contemporary politicians. But it is the concept of cooperative work groups that addresses the basic educational need of the students as they prepare for their entrance into the work force.

COMPONENTS OF THE COOPERATIVE WORK GROUP CONCEPT

The cooperative work group concept modernizes the standard cooperative learning methodology for today's business environment. It involves the integration of three basic areas of education in an attempt to holistically develop the student to be an effective contributing member of the twenty-first century work force. The three basic components of this educational concept are

- *Cooperative Learning:* How the learning environment is constructed and how students work with others

- *The Multiple Intelligences* (brain research): How students can be assisted in reaching their full individual potential

- *The Internet:* How the information age can be integrated into the curriculum

These three components are intertwined within the cooperative work group concept (see Figure 1.1). Up to now, all three have been regularly taught or implemented in the school as separate entities, with minimal connectivity. In today's working place, however, all three are critical if our students are to be successful. A brief description of these three core components of the cooperative work group concept follows:

Figure 1.1   The Three Components of the Cooperative Work Group Concept

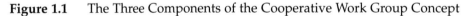

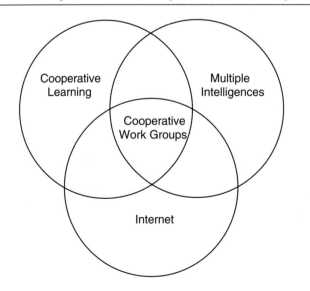

Cooperative Learning

This teaching methodology in its more advanced forms (Sharan, Shachar, & Levine, 1999; Sharan & Sharan, 1992) exemplifies the cooperative working environments found in today's business workplace better than any current teaching methodology (see Joyce, Calhoun, & Hopkins, 2002, and Joyce & Weil, 2000, for descriptions of the major models of teaching currently in use). Through the use of cooperative learning techniques, students learn how to accomplish curricular tasks, how to acquire high-level information and material in a positive, collaborative, interactive environment.

The Multiple Intelligences

Brain-based research—how students best learn—has become one of the most promoted topics in today's educational world (see Checkley, 1997). One of the most popular and useful manifestations of this research is the concept of the multiple intelligences (Gardner, 1999, 1993). The multiple intelligences examine how students best learn—how their brains efficiently acquire curricular material. By studying multiple intelligences, teachers can adapt their learning environment to make the learning process more efficient for each individual, thereby increasing a student's knowledge in a shorter period of time. If students with particular learning styles are matched to the tasks of the group, the requirements of individual work groups can be met better and more efficiently.

The Internet

The world is in a technological age. Today one needs to know not only how to operate this technology, but how to integrate its vast resources directly into one's work environment. In other words, one must acquire a degree of literacy in the digital world (Glister, 1997). Information and curricular material that once took hours, days, or weeks to acquire is now accessible electronically within seconds or minutes. In the information age it is incumbent upon both teachers and students to know how to locate and access that material quickly and efficiently and how to integrate it directly into their work.

COOPERATIVE WORK GROUPS

The cooperative work group concept integrates cooperative learning, the multiple intelligence, and the Internet into a learning environment that

- Prepares the students for the twenty-first century workplace
- Emphasizes the students' best individual learning style
- Integrates the newest technology into the students' work

John Dewey (1933, 1959) was the first to stress the importance of active student participation in learning experiences—an idea that became a central component of his philosophy. Ralph Tyler, elaborating on this concept when writing his curricular framework, stated, "Learning takes place through the active behavior of the student; it is what he or she does that is learned, not what the teacher does" (Tyler, 1949, p. 63). This is the core philosophy of the developers of cooperative learning.

Cooperative learning, although developed in the 1950s by Herbert Thelen (1954), has been widely implemented and researched only since the 1970s. In this methodology, students' active learning time in a cooperative learning unit or lesson exceeds that of most "traditional" methods of teaching (Slavin, 1995)—an important variable in student educational success (Fenstermacher, 1985; Harnischfeger & Wiley, 1976, 1985). Cooperative learning's successes have been well documented, showing how this method holds significant potential for improving student performance, peer group and interracial relations, and self-esteem (Johnson & Johnson, 1986, 1999; Sharan, 1994; Sharan et al., 1984; Slavin, 1995).

The methodology has also been shown to be extremely effective in teaching students higher-level skills (Joyce, Showers, & Rolheiser-Bennett, 1987). This is especially true when one wants students to think divergently, work together to generate and test hypotheses, reason causally, master complex bodies of information, and analyze social situations, and to develop flexible social skills—all crucial abilities for success in today's business climate (Joyce, 1985; Joyce & Calhoun, 1996, 1998).

It is important to note that the cooperative work group concept is *not* a rehashing of the cooperative learning emphasized throughout the educational world in the 1980s and 1990s. Rather, it draws important components from that teaching methodology and builds upon them in order to construct a new learning environment for today's students. Unlike most traditional cooperative learning lessons presently used (see Johnson & Johnson, 1986, 1999; Kagan, 1989; Slavin, 1995; Slavin, Madden, & Stevens, 1989), cooperative work group projects are long-term events. The overall learning experience will normally last anywhere from a few days to a few weeks— very similar to real life in the modern business world, where most projects tend to be conducted on a long-term basis.

The cooperative work group differs from the normative cooperative learning group in that it is not just a group of students arbitrarily placed together for a specific limited lesson. Rather, a cooperative work group takes on a "culture" of its own that allows it to work successfully and productively over an extended period of time, for example, teacher long-term committees or study groups. Over a period of time, the group begins to function as a particular entity, where the work dynamics and relationships become "standardized." The members act, communicate, and work together in certain ways, many of which eventually become predictable. As these mores become established, a lasting group becomes productive in its own right. Long-term student cooperative work groups evolve in much the same fashion.

An extensive amount of research into the function of groups was conducted in the 1970s and 1980s in the business community (see Hackman, 2002, and Hackman, Lawler, & Porter, 1983). Much of this literature is directly pertinent to features of the cooperative work group process.

For instance, Hare (1976) concluded that there are five basic characteristics of cooperative work groups that distinguish them from typical cooperative learning groups:

- The members of the group are in *interaction* with one another.
- They share a common *goal.*
- They share a set of *norms.*
- They develop a set of *roles.*
- They develop a network of interpersonal attraction, which serves to differentiate them from other groups. (p. 5)

Hare's basic assumptions are relevant to cooperative work group experiences today. These five important characteristics, when taken together, create a productive, functioning, long-term working group. The following section looks at each characteristic individually:

The members of the group are in interaction with one another. The members of a cooperative work group interact on a continuous basis, discussing options and ideas, planning for future actions, and sharing material and experiences together as a unit. Cooperative work group members are not simply students sitting together as individuals working on an assignment. Nor are they students who are tutoring one another in a way where information flows in one direction, from one student to another.

They share a common goal. In a well-functioning cooperative work group, the members share common goals. They are working together on a project, or on an aspect of it, the performance tasks of which have been agreed upon by all the members. For the most part, they share the same motivation—extrinsic or intrinsic—which assists them in reaching their goals.

They share a set of norms. Cooperative work group members share a set of norms. As the group begins to function on a long-term basis, certain behaviors—working and communicating—are accepted or rejected. Norms are established. These norms may be explicitly stated or, more often, implicitly implied. These norms change from group to group and project to project, depending on the individual composition and dynamics of that particular unit.

They develop a set of roles. Cooperative work groups develop naturally a set of roles within the group. This is in direct opposition to the traditional concept of distributed leadership and roles within cooperative learning groups (a topic discussed in Chapter 4). Group leadership naturally develops, and the members begin to fill certain "niches" in the group's dynamics.

They develop a network of interpersonal attraction, which serves to differentiate them from other groups. Probably the most important aspect of cooperative work groups is that over time, the members develop a network of interpersonal attraction that serves to differentiate them from other groups. The group begins to assume a "personality" of its own, one that is different from every other group that is working on the same project, or that works together at other times. The individual members become "seasonings," where each individual's unique personal characteristics (seasoning) when "mixed" together with those of the others in the group creates a special, highly unique "entree" that is different from all others. In a well-functioning cooperative work group, there is a noticeable change in the group dynamics of a work session whenever a member is missing—regardless of who that member might be.

All successful cooperative work groups have these five characteristics. The degree to which they are fully developed and manifested within the confines of the classroom curricula is determined by the special skills and planning of the particular teacher.

Cooperative work groups are designed to function productively on long-term projects—those covering days or even weeks. Consequently, the teacher needs to be considerably more attentive to the composition of the groups—much more so than for a typical, short-term, one-day cooperative learning project. As in the adult business world, the individuals in the groups need to be able to work together in reaching the project goals.

Hare (1976) pointed out that in order for a group to survive over time as a functioning, useful unit, it must meet four basic needs:

- The members must share a common identity and have a commitment to the values of the group.

- They must have or be able to generate the skills and resources necessary to reach the group goals.

- They must have rules that allow them to coordinate their activity and enough feeling of solidarity to stay together to complete the task.

- They must provide enough leadership and control to be effective in reaching their goal. (p. 17)

Inherent in these basic survival needs are various elements of social interaction. The interaction of the personalities of the group members, in conjunction with the environment in which the group operates, has a direct relationship to the way the group functions as a unit. Hare put these various factors together in graphic form:

Figure 1.2   Personality and Environmental Influences on Groups

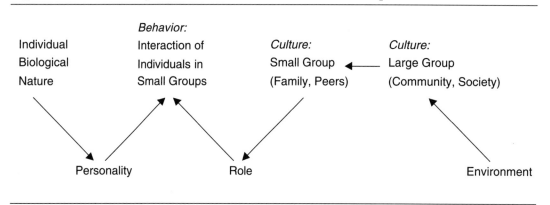

SOURCE: Hare, 1976, p. 4

A large amount of research in the business world has also been conducted concerning the various roles that individuals take when they are operating in a small group. Beebe and Masterson (1999) reported that depending on one's personality, and on the requirements of the group at that specific time, there are various roles that people naturally assume within the group. They published a comprehensive list of the possible roles that manifest themselves during the course of the group's work. Beebe and Masterson categorized them into three sections (see Figure 1.3. For a detailed explanation of the functions of each role, see Beebe & Masterson, 1999).

The group process is extremely complicated, especially when dealing with long-term projects such as those promoted in the cooperative work group concept.

Figure 1.3 Roles in Small Groups

Group Task Roles	Group Building and Maintenance Roles	Individual Roles
Initiator-Contributor	Encourager	Aggressor
Information-seeker	Harmonizer	Blocker
Opinion-seeker	Compromiser	Recognition-seeker
Information-giver	Gatekeeper & expediter	Self-confessor
Opinion-giver	Standard-setter	Playboy
Elaborator	Group observer	Dominator
Coordinator	Follower	Help-seeker
Orientor		Special interest pleader
Evaluator-critic		
Energizer		
Procedural technician		
Recorder		

SOURCE: Beebe and Masterson, 1982, pp. 59–61

Not every individual can, or does, fit every role. There are other outside variables that determine not only the roles one takes in a group, but how one operates within that role, at that particular moment in time.

Hare (1976) wrote that small-group research in the business community most often reports on the existence of six major areas and their factors that influence the group process:

- *Personality:* Intelligence, adjustment (anxiety), extroversion-introversion, dominance, masculinity-femininity, radicalism-conservatism, interpersonal sensitivity. (pp. 181–199)

- *Social Characteristics:* Age, sex, physical attractiveness, physical handicaps, social class, ethnicity, friendship group, birth order. (pp. 200–213)

- *Group Size:* Optimum number is five (strict deadlocks can be avoided and members can shift roles quickly); problems with groups of three, even-number groups, and larger groups. (pp. 214–231)

- *Task:* Kind of task (goal), criteria for task completion, rules (or roles) that must be followed, method of imposing the rules, amount of stress on the members, consequences of failure or success. (pp. 232–259)

- *Communication Network:* Seating patterns that lead to communication patterns that subsequently enhance or hinder each individual's communication contribution. (pp. 260–277)

- *Leadership:* Depends on the needs of the group and the personalities of the members; potential leaders usually receive higher ratings than others on *traits* such as intelligence, enthusiasm, dominance, self-confidence, and social participation. (pp. 278–303)

Hare maintained that the greatest problems facing groups were those dealing with the balance between group and individual concerns. Once these are all adequately dealt with (and no extenuating circumstances arise in any of the factors listed above), one usually develops an effective group.

Much of the previously cited research from the business community is directly applicable to the cooperative work group concept in the classroom. The development of the group as a specific, functioning unit, and the role of individuals—their personalities, abilities, and characteristics—directly influence the success of the cooperative work group experience. How a teacher deals with, and plans for, these student and environmental variables is discussed in the following chapters.

THE SCOPE OF THIS BOOK

This book is designed to assist current and future teachers with the planning and implementation of successful cooperative work group experiences from kindergarten through twelfth grade, in all core subjects (Language Arts/English, History/Social Studies, Science, and Mathematics). In order to attain this goal, the material has been organized in this fashion:

Part I: The Way Students Accomplish Tasks deals with the characteristics of cooperative learning, particularly group investigation, that are integrated into the cooperative work group concept. The chapters begin with a discussion of how cooperative work groups use an advanced, contemporary form of cooperative learning. This latest classroom research is then applied in a scenario of a teacher dealing with the most important components of the methodology: group formation, the leadership variable, acquiring curricular materials, and the teacher's role—promoting critical thinking implementing good classroom management and assessment techniques.

Part II: The Way Students Learn Effectively and Efficiently discusses the concept of the multiple intelligences and how to implement them in the classroom. The chapters begin with a discussion of this current form of brain research. The discussion then turns to how, in general terms, use of the multiple intelligences can be beneficial to teachers. The chapters then become more specific by actually planning the use of the multiple intelligences in one's present curriculum, to reviewing how to integrate them into cooperative work group experiences, plus how to use this new, modern philosophy in solving student learning problems.

Part III: The Internet as the Ultimate Teacher Resource Center starts with a discussion of the concept of digital literacy, which entails the need to become literate and comfortable in today's technological, information-based world. The chapters discuss the societal pressures that teachers address when implementing technology within their curricula in an environment with limited educational funding. The chapters conclude by reviewing the practical, easy, and efficient ways a teacher may locate virtually any curricular material on the Internet, and integrate it into the cooperative work group experience, even when there is limited Internet access within the school environment.

Part IV: Some Practical Examples of Cooperative Work Groups in Action contains a number of lessons created by classroom teachers that exemplify the material and concepts presented in this book. These lessons cover all four core subject areas and grade levels, and are meant to demonstrate how to pattern one's own planning and initial use of the cooperative work group concept.

The book ends with a number of Resources and References to further help the present or future teacher in creating and implementing successful cooperative work group experiences within the present classroom curricula.

NOTES

1. All Internet sites within the text (unless they are a direct quote from an online source) are represented in capital letters, with their URLs listed in Resource A. This saves the text from being cluttered with the long lists of letters and numbers common to Internet addresses.

2. See Nelson and Watras, 1981, for a review of the scientific movement in education in the early twentieth century and its origins in the scientific management and industrial efficiency theories of Frederich Taylor.

Part I

The Way Students Accomplish Tasks

An Advanced, Modern Form of Cooperative Learning

The concept of cooperative work groups acquires its roots in the group investigation model of cooperative learning—a teaching methodology that implements long-term projects involving student problem solving. Current research into student learning styles and teacher interaction has been integrated into the model, resulting in the development of this new material on cooperative work groups.

The group investigation model was developed in detail by the Sharans in the 1980s (Sharan, 1994; Sharan & Sharan, 1992; Sharan et al., 1984), based on the original work of Thelan (1954, 1960). What particularly distinguished this particular teaching methodology from the various models of Slavin (Slavin, 1995; Slavin et al., 1989), the Johnsons (1986), or Kagan (1989), is that unlike most representative classroom cooperative learning situations, which may last a few hours at most, in group investigation, students typically work on projects that range from short term (a few days) to long term (weeks or months). This extended interactive experience is the type of cooperative work group situation that most resembles the requirements of today's business (see Carnevale, 1996, 1991; Carnevale & Porro, 1994; Carnevale, Gainer, & Meltzer, 1990).

In the business world, projects are rarely conducted or concluded within a couple of hours. On the contrary, a business cooperative work group may be in operation over a period of years, depending on the scale of the particular project. The ability to function successfully and efficiently within a long-term cooperative work situation is a critical skill for students to learn if they are to be active, successful participants in the twenty-first century American economy.

This section is *not* a text devoted to the teaching of a particular cooperative learning model. There are numerous other books that review in great detail how one uses those various teaching methodologies. Rather, the focus of this text is the adaptation of the core components of the group investigation method of cooperative learning to the typical classroom as part of the cooperative work group concept. However, it is important for the reader to review the fundamental stages involved in this methodology prior to the discussion.

According to Joyce and Weil (2000) in *Models of Teaching,* there are six basic phases in the group investigation model:

Phase 1: Students encounter puzzling situation (planned or unplanned). The students must feel that there is some type of "problem" that needs to be solved by their investigation.

Phase 2: Students explore reactions to the situation. The class as a whole discusses the variables involved in the problem and possible avenues to investigate.

Phase 3: Students formulate study task and organize for study (problem definition, role, assignments, etc.). The students then are divided into cooperative groups. The groups discuss and plan the scope and sequence of their own investigation, based on the parameters established by the initial class discussion and requirements.

Phase 4: Independent and group study. The students use the resources available to complete their part of the class investigation.

Phase 5: Students analyze progress and process. Each group's progress is discussed by the class as a whole.

Phase 6: Recycle activity. Based on the students' progress, the investigation is continued, adapted, or changed, and the activity is started once again upon conclusion.

Although this particular teaching model has proven highly successful (see Sharan, 1994; Sharan et al., 1984), there are certain facets of the methodology that are problematic when transferred to the adult business environment. For example, Thelan (1954, 1960) believed that the student groups were to be created according to the personal interests of the students. Unfortunately, in most instances, this is not the situation in the business world. Cooperative work groups that adults will be required to face are formulated on the tasks necessary for the completion of specific work objectives. Employees in the business arena are placed within groups based on job descriptions, personal skills, and the specific tasks required, not on their own personal interest. This is contrary to current Cooperative Learning practices, where the students are regularly placed within groups that they individually select.

Another problem exists with the group investigation model—it is *completely* student centered. The teacher assumes a purely secondary role. Even Joyce and Weil (2000) categorize the group investigation model as part of "The Social Family" of curricular methodologies, with the social aspects—not the task—being the primary driving force. Again, this is not the type of work environment students will face when they enter the twenty-first century work world.

Traditional cooperative learning methodologies, including the group investigation model, have all primarily concentrated on the interaction of the members of the group as they attain a particular goal. Little emphasis is placed on the individual (other than as a component of the overall group), nor on the medium in which the tasks are accomplished. Whereas this methodology was a dramatic, and highly successful, departure from the "traditional" classroom of the twentieth century, it falls short of what is required of the workforce in the new millennium.

Although the previously sited research proved the overall success of cooperative learning, there were significant shortcomings when these data were applied to the average classroom. Unfortunately, the bulk of the research on this teaching methodology concentrated on the outcomes of the specific cooperative learning models, models that carry strict procedures for the teacher to follow, allowing limited deviation.

Little has been written on *why* or *how* cooperative learning works, or on core theoretical components that can be transferred to a variety of teaching situations.

This is a crucial omission, for every teaching situation is different—just as is every business. Rather than have the participants adapt their learning or teaching styles, individual personalities, and school environments to an outside instructional model, teachers and students need to know the basic concepts of "what works" within a cooperative work group experience. The specific six phases of the group investigation model enumerated above may not be appropriate for all cooperative work group situations. However, the basic, essential components of successful group investigation work can be adapted to all situations. It is on these general, applicable teaching components that this text now focuses.

The cooperative work group concept takes the fundamental components of cooperative learning and "modernizes" them for the requirements of the twenty-first century workplace. This is accompanied by the incorporation of brain-based research and the integration of new technology. The brain-based research, here taking the form of the multiple intelligences theory (Gardner, 1993), helps teachers determine the most efficient way in which their students learn. In other words, individual learning styles are dealt with in conjunction with the specific cooperative tasks of the group, thereby allowing the group to function more efficiently and productively. The integration of technology, in this case, the Internet, allows the students in the work groups to make use of the most modern, available resources in their pursuit of the group's tasks and goals. Both of these important areas—brain-based research and technology—are discussed in detail in subsequent chapters. For now, the discussion is directed to characteristics of the cooperative group work environment.

There are five basic components of the cooperative work group environment that are primary and integral in all classroom situations. These are not "phases" as enumerated in Joyce and Weil's research, but features of the cooperative work group philosophy that work together to provide a positive, successful learning experience:

1. Group Formation

How are the groups constructed?

This is the planning process in which the teacher engages to compose the most efficient groupings based on the goals of the experience.

2. Leadership

How does the group actually function, based on the specific leadership personalities of the participants?

This is a primary aspect of traditional cooperative learning that has been "mishandled" or ignored in the past.

3. Materials

How does the teacher supply the student groups with the materials required to accomplish the groups' goals?

This is the area where implementation of group investigation experiences has traditionally failed, for if there are insufficient materials, there can be no investigation.

4. Teacher Role: Critical Thinking and Classroom Management

How does the teacher interact with the students, and what is the impact of this on the groups' dynamics?

How can the groups function efficiently and successfully in an environment so foreign to the traditional classroom teaching methodology?

The first area—teacher interaction—is often ignored in the research on cooperative learning methodology, but has tremendous ramifications on the critical thinking levels of the students. Concerning the latter, success with classroom management issues can make or break cooperative learning projects for the entire year.

5. Assessment

How does the teacher assess whether or not the cooperative group experience was successful for both the individual students and the group as a whole?

This is an area that most concerns administrators, parents, and students, and must therefore be adequately addressed.

The subsequent chapters discuss how the teacher can successfully implement each of these important facets of the cooperative work group environment into a traditional classroom.

PUTTING THEORY INTO PRACTICE: HOW COULD THEY MAKE A DIFFERENCE?

Mr. Washington's American History students were discussing the period referred to as the "Gilded Age," particularly the problems that the new urbanization created at the turn of the twentieth century. Eventually, the classroom discussion led to a comparison of how societal problems were addressed then as compared to today. They discussed how cities became overcrowded, how there were virtually no health, safety, or child labor laws applicable to protect the worker, and that there were no social service organizations to assist those who found themselves out of work and destitute.

When the subject of the homeless in twenty-first century America was raised, the students discussed various efforts their own school had made on behalf of the homeless, in particular, a successful canned food drive the previous Thanksgiving. Mr. Washington pointed out how the homeless in our country eat fairly well during the holiday season, but often go hungry the remainder of the year. Noting that it was now March, each of the students in the class admitted that not one of them had made a contribution to the homeless since New Year's.

Mr. Washington then showed a videotape of some of the real, everyday stories presented on the Comic Relief broadcast—the semi-annual fund-raising drive for the homeless in America. The five-minute vignettes portrayed "normal" people, including children, who became homeless due to calamities such as unexpected unemployment, illness, or simply being evicted from an apartment. The broadcast interviews with school-age children and their parents dispelled the myth that the homeless were "bums," but were instead people just like the students.

Following this emotional experience, the students decided that they wanted to make a difference in their society, that they wanted to do something to help the homeless in their community.

Mr. Washington's class chose to create a schoolwide awareness campaign to move the concept of helping the homeless from a "special-event" status (i.e., the annual food drive) to one of an everyday activity in their lives. They determined that their project would take two forms. First, the students decided that they would present a schoolwide assembly, the goal of which was to introduce and inform the student body of the overall problem. In turn, they would also create and provide everyone with an original "Help the Homeless" brochure—a "handbook" or reference that students would use throughout the year to make an individual difference in their community.

With their solution to this problem basically designed, Mr. Washington's students then decided to break up into cooperative work groups, with each group taking on one particular aspect of the project. The following describes the five different groups and the work that they accomplished:

- *Drama Group.* This group was charged with the responsibility to create and present a short play highlighting the plight of the homeless. They first went online and did a METACRAWLER[1] search using the term *homeless* and received sixty-two different links to Internet sites containing relevant information. Using the data provided on these sites, they were able to acquire the material needed for their play, which was produced and practiced by the group and presented at the all-school assembly.

- *Music Group.* This group's responsibility was to create and present a song, using original lyrics, that also highlighted the plight of the homeless. They also went online and used some of the information that the Drama Group had located. They then rewrote the lyrics to the song "God Help the Outcasts" (Menken & Schwartz, 1996). The group learned, choreographed, and presented it during the assembly.

- *Literature Group.* This group developed a few personal anecdotes for both the assembly and the "Help the Homeless" brochure by using the same Internet sites discovered above, along with material gleaned from the Comic Relief shows.

- *Brochure Group (Investigation).* Again, using the Internet links previously discovered, plus the local telephone directory, this group researched and identified the various homeless agencies within their city. They organized the information into the following categories: address, telephone number, hours of operation, type of services offered, and initial contact person. Most important, they also investigated what a person their age could individually do to assist these agencies.

- *Brochure Group (Publication).* This group first collected and investigated various types of brochures used to disseminate information. Then the students designed, typed, and constructed the "Help the Homeless" brochure that was distributed to the entire student body.

Ultimately, through the use of a cooperative work group experience incorporating Internet resources and a variety of presentation modes, Mr. Washington's class created and produced an extremely successful program addressing the problem of how students can help with the homeless in their community.

NOTE

1. All Internet sites in the text (unless they are within a direct quote from an online source) are represented in capital letters, with their URLs listed in Resource A. This saves the text from being cluttered with the long lists of letters and numbers common to Internet addresses.

Group Formation

2

The first crucial variable in ensuring successful cooperative work groups is the way in which the students are organized. The composition and size of the unit can readily enhance or sabotage the overall goals of the learning experience. Short-term groups (groups lasting for less than a day) can be assigned on the spot—for example, having three students who sit next to each other engage in a quick assignment. When "study"-type groups are composed prior to a test, the teacher can quickly and easily assign a high-, medium-, and low-achieving student with minimal thought or analysis to a group. In contrast, the long-term groups that are required when conducting extensive cooperative work group projects need to be carefully formulated, which is directly related to teacher planning.

The first decision that the teacher makes is to determine the optimum size of the student groups, with the ideal size of a cooperative work group being composed of four to six members. This variable is partially determined by the tasks that are required for the learning experience. Groups with fewer or greater numbers often result in a dysfunctional unit. There are a number of variables to consider when determining the size of the groups:

• *Three-person groups* are the most problematic ones. Decisions in these groups inevitably are made based on social considerations—a "two versus one" situation where two band together rather than making decisions as a result of the data presented in the group discussion.

• *A group with seven or more members* frequently becomes unwieldy due to the large number of opinions that need to be heard on the issues at hand. In other words, it may transform the group into a "committee." (Remember the old riddle: "What's a camel?" "A horse developed by a committee.")

• *Four- to six-member groups* are manageable and allow for the diversity to adequately address most project issues. An even number of members is actually an asset. Most teachers seem to shy away from having an even number of students in a group (reasoning that votes within the unit could inevitably result in a tie). When group "votes" have to be decided by a significant consensus rather than a one-vote margin, it leads to stronger decision-making process.

Once the overall structure of the group has been established, the actual composition of the membership is determined chiefly by the goals for that particular learning activity. From where do one's goals derive? Either state or district educational standards.

This has become a central aspect for all educational planning today, and a discussion that goes beyond the scope of this book. As with all curricular planning, when formulating cooperative work group experiences, the central basis is that all goals must be rooted within predetermined educational standards.

Cooperative group work goals primarily revolve around three basic curricular scenarios:

- *The students are to learn specific curricular material.*

  This is the scenario when all students are expected to learn from the experience the same particular body of knowledge.

- *The students are to learn supplemental or varying material on a topic.*

  This is when students either have the option to choose the areas that interest their group, or when each group is assigned a specific, different task for the overall classroom investigation.

- *The students are to address a classroom social issue or problem.*

  This is essentially determined by the aggregation of students within the class, particularly if the class is heterogeneously mixed by nonacademic criteria such as socioeconomic status, ethnic/racial mix, or social status within the school. This is the situation when the teacher primarily wants students representative of different groups to work together as a cooperative group to become socially closer. The curricular material that is to be covered is secondary to the social and affective goals that are to be achieved. However, even though the academic goals are secondary, there must be relevant and appropriate curricular material for the group to research, investigate, and manipulate, to function appropriately.

Research has continually demonstrated that cooperative learning significantly raises students' academic and social gains in the majority of educational situations in which it is implemented (Slavin, 1995). Be that as it may, in order to ensure maximum gains, the grouping of the students should still be determined by the teacher's primary educational goals, as listed above. Different levels and priorities of academic and social goals inevitably exist for every conceivable grouping situation, and in every potential lesson. However, the fundamental curricular aspect of the learning experience should guide the teacher, for group composition will vary greatly depending on this primary, core goal. For instance:

- *If the teacher's primary goal is for the students to learn specific curricular material,* then each group must be heterogeneously mixed determined by reading level and academic achievement. Each group's composition must allow the members equal access to the material, and equal opportunity for the successful learning and acquisition of that particular material. Therefore, personality and social conflicts among the students should be avoided at all costs as they will almost surely lead to academic disruptions within the cooperative work group. This is definitely not the time for peer group experimentation.

- *If the teacher's primary goal is for the students to learn supplemental or ancillary material on a topic,* then the group needs to be heterogeneously mixed determined by the material to be used. If reading is required, then adequate readers need to be present in each. If artwork is involved, then those with a high spatial multiple intelligence should be included in each group. (Refer to Part II for a discussion of the

Figure 2.1 Matching the Teacher's Goals to the Needs of the Group

Primary Goal	*Needs of the Group*
The students are to learn specific curricular material	The group should be heterogeneous, based on academic ability. The group must have at least one student who can handle the reading level of the material to be studied by the group.
The students are to learn supplemental or varying material on a topic	The group should be heterogeneously mixed according to the needs of the cooperative group work experience. Multiple intelligences can be applied as a supplemental determinant.
The teacher wants to address a classroom social issue or problem among the students	The group should be organized by bringing together those to whom the problem is addressed. The group must have members capable of working successfully with the required curricular material.

multiple intelligences as they relate to group work.) Minor personality and social conflicts can be integrated into the group, if they do not significantly interfere with the group's overall progress.

- *If the teacher's goal is for the students to address a classroom social issue or problem among the students,* then the students should be divided into the appropriate groups designed to address the issue. However, the teacher still must be cognizant of the curricular work and material with which the group will be engaging, to ensure that they are capable of successfully completing their tasks; for example, if reading material is required, then competent readers must be in each group, otherwise academic failure could cause social failure and the teacher's goal would not be accomplished.

Figure 2.1 provides a brief summary of these three significant grouping variations.

Once the goals have been established, the teacher needs to take into account any special needs that may ultimately affect the learning experience for the students. Although a large number of educational variables exist within each classroom, there are four basic common areas, any of which, if not adequately addressed, could seriously affect the success of cooperative work group situations. (Important student personality variables such as "leadership" and "nonparticipation" are discussed in a subsequent section.) These four categories include:

- Readers
- Special education students
- English language learner (ELL) students[1]
- Student Internet access

As discussed above, when formulating groups, a teacher needs to be aware of both the individual student's reading levels and of the reading level required by the curricular material to be investigated. Students not able to read and understand the material that needs to be incorporated within the group's work assignment become frustrated. This problem inevitably will sabotage the groups' overall accomplishments. However, this can be avoided with advanced planning as follows:

- When there are a significant number of nonreaders within the classroom, each cooperative work group must have at least one reader who can handle the required material. The group can then still adequately function. The group is to function holistically as a single unit, versus "x" number of individuals placed together. One student's role can be to read the more difficult material to, or for, the group, and extract and/or summarize the pertinent information.

- The teacher can search the Internet to locate material on the subject of the investigation at the most appropriate level for the students. (See Part III for a complete discussion on how to locate curricular materials on the Internet.)

Numerous studies have demonstrated that special education students are easily, and successfully, mainstreamed into cooperative learning groups (Slavin, 1995). During the group formation process, they need to be distributed among the other students, depending on both their particular disabilities and strengths. Mainstreamed special education students cover a wide spectrum of disabilities, ranging from those who function perfectly with slight behavioral modifications, to those who require a one-on-one aide. The crucial determination for the teacher is discovering what modifications, if any, are needed for the students' successful integration into the cooperative work group experience. Once the modifications are implemented, the special education students will be full, contributing members of the group.

There are a number of ways to ensure that special education students can have a favorable, meaningful, and rewarding experience in a cooperative group work situation. For example:

- If the special education students are nonreaders, partner with readers.

- If they have social or emotional problems, partner with those with whom they get along.

- Most important, the teacher must also assure that the groups are required to perform certain tasks in which these students can inevitably succeed (e.g., nonreading special education students should not be in a group activity where all investigation, tasks, and reporting are dependent on higher level reading abilities. That situation is sure to lead to failure, social stigma, or at the very least, a critical drop in the students' self-esteem as they become "useless" to the group.).

The teacher must ensure that mainstreamed special education students are balanced among the groups and are made to feel useful. In fact, when necessary modifications have been addressed, special education students in cooperative groups often use each other's strengths and become full and equal working members with the other students.

ELL students can also become full members of any group when their language restrictions are directly addressed. The primary rule for all teachers to remember, and a critical distinction that one must always keep in mind, is that deficiencies in English literacy are not automatically correlated to deficiencies in cognitive ability.

First and foremost, when working with ELL students, the teacher needs to determine if the lesson is to be primarily a "content-based" lesson or an "English" lesson. This is a critically important distinction. Virtually all lessons are "English" lessons at some level, and if the goal of the cooperative group experience is primarily subject matter, content-based, then there is absolutely nothing wrong with allowing ELL students to work in their native language, and therefore become full members of the group. This can be accomplished in one of two ways:

- If there are a limited number of students speaking one language, or if limited curricular material exists in that language, then the ELL student should be automatically paired with an English-fluent student who also speaks that particular language. The English-fluent student serves as a "translator" throughout the group experience, allowing the ELL student to participate cognitively in all facets of the group work.

- Second, if enough students in the classroom speak the same language, they can be organized into a group and be allowed to work, discuss, and present their work, using higher-order critical thinking skills, in their own primary language. Much of their research can be conducted in their primary language as there is a growing amount of material available on the Internet from foreign countries. How to locate these sites is discussed in full in Part III.

If the teacher's primary goal is for the students to acquire subject-matter curricular information, versus an English development goal, then the students should be in a situation that allows for cognitive development and participation without the constraints of limited language skills. Again, group composition directly follows the determination of the teacher's specific goals.

Student Internet accessibility is the fourth category, and is a new teacher concern. It has become a critical variable in the twenty-first century work place and educational setting. Internet resources are now becoming an important aspect of

Box 2.1 Having High Expectations for All Students

Teacher Expectations and ELL Students: The Self-Fulfilling Prophecy at Work

One of the most frustrating professional experiences I have ever had concerned an inservice workshop I attended. My large, urban district had just adopted a new state history series. We were required to learn how to teach the series by attending workshops led by a number of teachers who had already completed this curricular training.

The sixth-grade teacher leading our group was demonstrating how we could integrate a language arts activity into the unit on Ancient Egypt. One lesson involved how the students could "write postcards home from ancient Egypt." As she held up an example, she explained the activity in this fashion: "Your gifted students can fill up both sides of a postcard with material. Your Spanish-speaking students can write one or two sentences in Spanish."

It was the one time in my professional career that I ever interrupted a workshop leader. I immediately stood up and stated that if we are allowing students who have an English language deficiency to communicate in their native language, then the expectations for these students should be just as high as for those who are fluent in English.

This is a crucial concept to keep in mind as you are working with ELL students in cooperative group work situations. If the students are allowed to work in their native language, then the expectations should be just as high as for those who operate in English. Language deficiencies are not synonymous with cognitive deficiencies! The self-fulfilling prophecy is an overwhelming determinant to student success. High student expectations lead to greater student achievement. Low student expectations lead to lesser student achievement. Therefore, the teacher should expect ELL students to perform academically at the appropriate grade level once the language barrier has been adequately addressed.

grouping, because online resources are an integral part of the modern cooperative work group experience (see Part III for a full discussion of this area).

Access to the Internet within the classroom and/or school is, unfortunately, more often than not limited. The importance of the Internet access variable is dependent on the specific educational environment and on the socioeconomic status of the school community. For example, if all cooperative group work is to be accomplished at school, then this variable becomes irrelevant because it pertains to grouping procedures if there are computers (as no online activity occurs in the students' homes). However, if the teacher expects the students to conduct some portion of their group investigative work outside of the school, then it behooves the teacher to make sure that there are students in each group who have Internet access at home.

It is incumbent upon the teacher to determine the percentage of students who have home access to the Internet. This information should be periodically collected and recorded in an unobtrusive manner in the teacher's roll book throughout the year. This can be accomplished through including a confidential question, such as, "Do you have Internet access at home?" on the bottom of an assignment, rather than asking for a public "show of hands." Socioeconomic status usually determines Internet accessibility at home, and therefore, to make a "public display" of "haves" and "have-nots" could lead to personal embarrassment and other significant social problems and among the students.

Finally, after all of these variables have been adequately addressed, the teacher needs to organize the groups. The easiest way to accomplish this is through the use of a "grouping worksheet." A grouping worksheet is a grid that the teacher can quickly create based on the activity planned. On the top of the grid, the teacher determines the number of groups. Along the side, the teacher notes the number of students in the group and the basic grouping determinant, such as grades or reading ability. Figure 2.2 contains two examples of this grouping worksheet.

The teacher then progresses through the roll book and fills out the chart in pencil, to accommodate potential future changes. Students are then assigned to one group or another depending on an additional number of variables, such as:

- *Gender/race/ethnicity.* Ensuring that boys and girls of all categories are represented within each group

- *Social considerations.* Ensuring that close friends or those who have significant problems with each other are not assigned to the same group, unless relevant to the teacher's primary goals

- *Special needs.* Ensuring that ELL or special education partners are together, or other group considerations (as discussed above) are made

- *Internet usage.* Ensuring that each group has at least one student with Internet access at home, if this is appropriate for the task

- *Multiple intelligences.* Ensuring that each group has a variety of the multiple intelligences represented (discussed in full in Part II), or those specific intelligence requirements for that group

As the teacher gets to know the students during the year, this process gradually requires less time. Often the groups can be determined within a couple of minutes. A sixth important variable, leadership abilities, is discussed in detail in the next chapter.

Figure 2.2   Grouping Worksheets

Seven Groups, Heterogeneously Mixed as Determined by Grades on Their Last Test

Group #, Grade on Last Test	1	2	3	4	5	6	7
A							
B							
C							
D/F							

Five Groups, Heterogeneously Mixed as Determined by Reading Ability

Group #, Basic Reading Level	1	2	3	4	5
High					
Average					
Average					
Average					
Low					

Figure 2.3 Mr. Washington's Working Groups

Group[1]	Number	Minimum Requirements for Each Group's Membership
Drama	6–7	Grade-level readers needed. High bodily-kinesthetic MI Student home Internet access needed
Music	6–7	Grade-level readers needed High musical, bodily-kinesthetic MI Student home Internet access beneficial
Literature	6–7	Strong readers needed Linguistic MI Student home Internet access needed
Brochure Group (Investigation)	6–7	Grade-level readers needed Logical-mathematical, naturalist MI Student home Internet access needed
Brochure Group (Publication)	6–7	Grade-level readers needed Spatial MI

NOTE: 1. See earlier anecdote for a description of the tasks of each of these groups.

The important point for the teacher to remember is that care and consideration must be given to the formation of the student groups if a long-term successful cooperative work group experience is to result.

PUTTING THEORY INTO PRACTICE: MR. WASHINGTON'S COOPERATIVE WORK GROUPS

As a working example of these grouping procedures, please refer back to Mr. Washington's cooperative work group experience in the opening anecdote. During the planning stages of this project it was determined that this was going to be an extended learning experience. Therefore, he took extra care in the formation of the student groups.

The first step Mr. Washington took was to determine his primary goal for the group experience, which was for the students to learn supplemental or varying material on a topic. With thirty-two students in his class, he knew that he could form five working groups of six or seven students. This would basically keep him within the grouping guidelines, although he was aware that two groups would be slightly larger. He decided that he would carefully observe those two groups, and if they became unwieldy, split them into "subgroups."

Mr. Washington then reviewed each of the projected group tasks, determining the student qualifications needed for their successful completion. He determined that the most important variables involved reading level, multiple intelligence, and student Internet access. Figure 2.3 displays the various requirements for each of the projected groups, as determined by Mr. Washington.

Figure 2.4 Washington's First Grouping Worksheet

Student Qualities	Groups				
	Drama	Music	Literature	Brochure (Investigation)	Brochure (Publication)
Name Reader?[1] High MI[2] Internet	Ilya Yes Bodily-kinesthetic	Freddy Yes Musical	Ashlee Yes Linguistic Yes	Melvin Yes Logical-mathematical Yes	Gaby Yes Spatial
Name Reader? High MI Internet	Stephanie Yes Bodily-kinesthetic Yes	Cari Yes Bodily-kinesthetic	Laura Yes Yes	Jeremy Yes	Carla Yes Spatial Yes
Name Reader? High MI Internet	Jesenia Bodily-kinesthetic Yes	Sally Musical	Elizabeth Linguistic	Olivia Naturalist	Seth Spatial
Name Reader? High MI Internet	Tatyanna Bodily-kinesthetic	Josh Yes	Raul Linguistic	Andrew Logical-mathematical Yes	Ronny Spatial
Name Reader? High MI Internet	Nancy	Shannon Musical Yes	Karen Linguistic	Katrina Logical-mathematical	Megan Spatial
Name Reader? High MI Internet	Mark Yes	Gordan Musical	Sean	Michael	Manuel Yes
Name Reader? High MI Internet	Alberto		Daniel Yes		

NOTES: 1. "Yes" denotes a student reading at grade level or above.

2. This is their highest multiple intelligence (MI) as it pertains to the assigned group. Many of these students had additional high areas that are not applicable here.

Upon studying his plan, Mr. Washington determined that it was not necessary for every member to have each characteristic listed for that particular group. However, in order for the cooperative work group to function at optimum efficiency, some of the students needed to exhibit those traits, so that each variable was represented within the unit.

Once the requirements were determined, Mr. Washington had to assign students to the various groups. Since there were a number of variables integrated within each of the group requirements, he decided to prioritize them to ensure that the most important factor for each group would be addressed. Keeping in mind the characteristics of his present students, he prioritized the grouping variables as follows:

- *First: Readers.* Ten of the thirty-two students read at grade level or above.

- *Second: Multiple intelligence levels.* An earlier classroom multiple intelligence test showed that he had enough students who were strong in the specific categories that he had noted. (See Part II for a full discussion how to determine and record students' multiple intelligences.)

- *Third: Student Internet access.* Twelve of his students had Internet access at home, as determined by an earlier private survey of the class.

- *Fourth: ELL students.* There were six students designated as ELL in the class.

- *Fifth: Special education students.* There were only two resource specialist students in his class, and both had functioned near grade level throughout the year. Consequently, this was not a significant factor.

Once the individual group requirements had been determined, and the priorities set, Mr. Washington went through his roll book and assigned students to the various groups. Figure 2.4 shows the grouping worksheet that he created.

Mr. Washington initially assigned students to the basic groups according to his goals and the needs of the groups. The next step was to take into account the leadership variable, one of the most important student variables in the cooperative group work experience.

NOTE

1. This term relates to all students who are not literate in the English language. Previously referred to as "ESL" (English as a Second Language), this category now also includes those who are native-born, but who are not yet literate in the English language. This is often the case with students whose primary language at home is not English.

Leadership 3

One of the most-often espoused tenets of successful cooperative group experiences was the need to distribute leadership among the members of the group (Slavin, 1995). However, subsequent research has demonstrated that this is a false assumption (Mandel, 1991). Leadership is a personality trait; people are on a "leadership continuum."[1] On one end, people enjoy and actively seek leadership within groups; on the opposite end, they strongly attempt to avoid it. This is true among adults on a committee, of college students required to participate in a classroom group project, and of school-age children assigned to a cooperative group. Some people love the interpersonal experience and gravitate to group leadership; some abhor it and will participate only when required to do so. When adults get together to work on a project, and leadership has not been predetermined through the identification of a "chairperson" or some other position, always one or more eventually "take over" and lead the group. There are also those who simply sit back and participate only when necessary. The same dynamic behaviors are found with groups of students.

When students are placed in cooperative work groups, all leadership behaviors will be inevitably displayed in one of the following four leadership categories:

Task Leadership

The student is concerned with activities involved in the actual group process—keeping others on task, getting supplies, and having questions answered (the process of answering, not the content of the answers).

Examples:

"We need to find out how the pioneers crossed the Mississippi River."

"Take out your papers."

"Go ask the teacher if we have to answer question number four."

Intellectual Leadership

The student offers a new idea to the group. (This is different from simply answering someone's question with information that was researched).

Examples:

"The pioneers built barges to float their wagons across the Mississippi River."

"I found out that they used coal to make the water hot enough to generate steam."

"You need to draw the border closer to the forty-fifth parallel, not the forty-fourth."

Social/Emotional Leadership

The student gives praise or encouragement—something construed as positive—to a member of the group.

Examples:

"You did a good job on that!"

"Thanks for getting that book."

"I love that pen! Where did you get it?"

Coercive Leadership

A student gives negative feedback or creates off-the-topic humor to disrupt the process, even momentarily.

Examples:

"That's stupid."

"Would you be quiet already!"

"I heard this joke . . ." (Mandel, 1998, p. 109).

Within these four different leadership categories, all of the students will also display one of three types of leadership style[2]:

Leaders. These students control all facets of the group and *initiate* virtually all dialogue between members.

Followers. These students readily answer questions and actively participate, but usually only at the instigation of one of the leaders.

Nonparticipants. These students never offer information unless asked; they never volunteer. However, they are rarely "off-task." They normally will complete whatever assignment is given to them. (Mandel, 1998, p. 109)

In the research on cooperative groups (Mandel, 1991), a fifth-grade classroom was videotaped during group work sessions for more than 40 hours during different stages of the school year. The results were rather startling. In every videotaped session when the cooperative groups worked together, regardless of the subject matter or varying group composition, *every* leadership position within the observed group was held by one of the students who were determined to be a "leader." It was irrelevant which of the four types of leadership categories were displayed—in fact, the leaders took turns at fulfilling different types of leadership roles, depending on who the other members of the group might have been at that particular time. Often a leader displayed more than one type of leadership role within the session. Sometimes a particular leadership category was held by more than one of the "leaders" within the group. However, *every* leadership position was assumed by a "leader" *every* time—a 100% positive correlation. Followers and nonparticipants *never* took a leadership position in any situation.

These data have serious and far-reaching implications for the teacher formulating extensive cooperative work group experiences. Previously cited research traditionally held that leadership in cooperative learning was to be "distributed," assigned among the group members on an equal, rotating basis. However, taken in light of the above study, if the concept of distributed leadership is in actuality practiced—where

Box 3.1

How Do You Determine Who Is a Leader?

A teacher can normally determine who are the major leaders and nonparticipants within a classroom during the first month of school. Some key signs include:

1. The leaders are the first ones to raise their hands in a discussion, and who consistently raise their hands when the teacher asks a question. They will also be among the first to raise their hands when another student is called upon, and does not know, or hesitates with, an answer. Be very careful, however, because this trait does not guarantee the correctness of the answers. Students with a strong leadership personality will try to answer continuously, even if they are aware that they probably do not know the correct answer. Quantity of volunteering, not quality, is the important variable.

2. At the end of class, as the students are gathering to leave, notice to whom they gravitate. These are generally the peer group leaders.

3. Observe the students in your class on the school grounds during nutrition/recess or lunch. Notice who is "in front" of the peer group as they move from one area to another. Who seems to make the decisions about where to go, and when?

These are just three of many ways a teacher can use to identify those in the class with the strongest leadership personality style. Remember the caution: leadership and cognitive ability are not synonymous! Many students who are considered "gang leaders" outside of class, or "delinquents" within the school, possess strong leadership personality traits but have not been able to succeed academically in school. These individuals have had to find a different, and ultimately negative, outlet for their leadership personality traits to manifest themselves.

It is important to recognize that students with a nonparticipant personality style are not "off-task" or slow. Many simply do not enjoy, or feel comfortable with, active participation in public with their peers, though they may be following and understanding every aspect of the lesson. Therefore, when teachers give a grade for "class participation," they are, in reality, evaluating whether or not a student has a leadership personality style, and not the student's attentiveness or cognitive participation.

the teacher insists that a nonleader take on a leadership role within the group—one of three potentially disruptive things will most likely occur:

- The leaders in the group will consciously, or subconsciously, assume the various leadership tasks from the nonleaders.

- The leaders in the group will sabotage the group through exerting negative/coercive leadership behavior (see definition above).

- The nonleaders become so uncomfortable, and suffer such cognitive dissonance with this leadership responsibility, that they will not be able to adequately function within the group, causing a leadership "vacuum."

In any event, the primary result will likely be that if leadership roles are arbitrarily assigned and enforced, the teacher will be left with a dysfunctional cooperative work group. Therefore, the teacher must be cognizant of the leadership styles of the students when formulating the groups. This may ultimately result in minor manipulations of the group's membership, once group formation has been initially completed.

The solution to the problems attributed to distributive leadership is relatively simple. Instead of distributing leadership, distribute *tasks*. At the beginning of a cooperative work group session, the teacher should discuss with the students what tasks need to be fulfilled. These could be as varied and typical as recorder, presenter, and materials-getter. The number and types of jobs is wholly dependent on both the group requirements integrated within the particular project, and the age of the students involved. The younger the students, the more the tasks may need to be defined and overtly stated. Older students will be more apt to naturally fulfill group requirements and roles. The group subsequently distributes the required tasks among the members, with the natural leadership of the students causing the group to operate smoothly.

Remember the introductory statements about the five characteristics of a work team (Hare, 1976)—the students need to develop their own particular culture, and develop their own set of roles within the group. These various roles should proceed naturally from the leadership personality traits of the cooperative work group members, rather than being arbitrarily assigned by the teacher.

PUTTING THEORY INTO PRACTICE: DISTRIBUTING THE LEADERS

Returning to our scenario with Mr. Washington's class, after Mr. Washington initially formed his groups, he looked over his roster concerning "leaders" and "nonparticipants" within the class. He had earlier in the year noted which of his students definitely fit within these two categories—those who continually initiated discussions and constantly attempted to participate, and those who rarely talked unless asked a question. The majority of the class, 22 students, fell within the "followers" category, and therefore, he did not note them especially in his role book.

The following students were determined to have a "leadership" personality style: Ashlee, Carla, Ilya, Laura, Mark, Melvin, and Stephanie.

The following students were determined to have a "nonparticipant" personality style: Alberto, Manuel, Nancy.

Figure 3.1   Washington's Final Grouping Worksheet, with Leadership Variable

Student Qualities	Groups				
	Drama	**Music**	**Literature**	**Brochure (Investigation)**	**Brochure (Publication)**
Name	Ilya	Freddy	Ashlee	Melvin	Gaby
Reader?	Yes	Yes	Yes	Yes	Yes
High MI[1]	Bodily-kinesthetic	Musical	Linguistic	Logical-mathematical	Spatial
Internet			Yes	Yes	
Leadership	Leader		Leader	Leader	
Name	Stephanie	Cari	Laura	Jeremy	Carla
Reader?	Yes	Yes	Yes	Yes	Yes
High MI	Bodily-kinesthetic	Bodily-kinesthetic			Spatial
Internet	Yes		Yes		Yes
Leadership	Leader		Leader		Leader
Name	Jesenia	Sally	Elizabeth	Olivia	Seth
Reader?					
High MI	Bodily-kinesthetic	Musical	Linguistic	Naturalist	Spatial
Internet	Yes				
Leadership					
Name	Tatyanna	Mark	Raul	Andrew	Ronny
Reader?					
High MI	Bodily-kinesthetic		Linguistic	Logical-mathematical	Spatial
Internet		Yes		Yes	
Leadership		Leader			
Name	Nancy	Shannon	Karen	Katrina	Megan
Reader?					Spatial
High MI		Musical	Linguistic	Logical-mathematical	
Internet		Yes			
Leadership	Nonparticipant				
Name	Josh	Gordan	Sean	Alberto	Manuel
Reader?					Yes
High MI		Musical			
Internet	Yes				
Leadership				Nonparticipant	Nonparticipant
Name	Michael		Daniel		
Reader?					
High MI					
Internet					
Leadership			Yes		

NOTE: 1. This is their highest multiple intelligence as it pertains to the assigned group. Many of these students had additional high areas, which are not listed here.

Studying his original grouping worksheet (see Figure 2.4), Mr. Washington noticed that one group (Drama) had three "leaders" assigned to it, while another group (Music) had no leaders. He also noticed that the Drama Group had two of the three "nonparticipants" within the group. Studying the various characteristics of the groups, and taking into account his prioritized list of student variables, he decided that he could easily switch Mark from the Drama Group with Josh in the Music Group, since both boys were not classified "readers," neither had a high applicable multiple intelligence (bodily-kinesthetic or musical), and both had Internet access at home. That switch would ensure that every group had at least one student who was classified as having a "leadership" personality style. In addition, Washington also determined that he could switch Alberto from the Drama Group with Michael in the Brochure (Investigation) Group since they, too, had the same student characteristics (nonreaders, no applicable high multiple intelligence, no home Internet access). With this alteration, no group would have more than one "nonparticipant" assigned.

By spreading out the leaders, followers, and nonparticipants, Mr. Washington was able to ensure that he would have better and more efficient working groups. Figure 3.1 is a display of the final grouping worksheet for this cooperative work group experience.

One final note about Mr. Washington's efforts. Whenever he creates a grouping worksheet, it is usually completed fairly quickly on simple, lined paper, versus the formalized charts displayed on these pages. As will be explained in Part II concerning the multiple intelligences, he has the following fundamental student characteristics noted in his roll book, some of which are applicable to this particular project, some not:

• Basic reading level (three categories: grade level & above/below grade level/ELL)

• Multiple intelligence strengths and weaknesses (one or two strongest areas, one or two weakest areas)

• Internet access at home (yes/no)

• Leadership level (strong display of leadership or nonparticipation styles)

• Gifted program (yes/no and specific area of designation)

• Special education program (including resource specialist pull-out)

• Takes the bus regularly (morning, afternoon, or both)

• Extracurricular school activities (organizations, clubs, etc.)

Each of these student variables is basically determined by Mr. Washington within the first month of school, and is noted in his roll book. Subsequently, it becomes quite easy for him to complete a grouping worksheet for his cooperative work groups in a minimal amount of time, by simply referring to his student notes.

NOTES

1. See Hackman, Lawler, and Porter (1983) for a full discussion on personality traits that affect behavior in organizations.

2. For a full discussion of how these categories were determined, see Mandel (1991).

Materials 4

The most significant problem involved with conducting a successful cooperative work group experience has absolutely nothing to do with the students or with the ultimate composition of the groups. Rather, it is related to the accessibility of the supplemental curricular materials needed to accomplish the tasks required of the project.

Nothing will sabotage a cooperative work group experience faster than having the students run out of materials to use in their investigation. Unfortunately, this occurs all too often as a direct result of restricted school supplementary material budgets that have been diminished over the past two decades, as the use of cooperative groups steadily increased. An encyclopedia and a classroom textbook are insufficient student resources for a successful cooperative learning experience that is expected to last more than an hour or two.

The Internet is rapidly proving to be the educational savior for teachers in this arena. An extensive discussion follows in Part III on how to locate curricular materials on the Internet. For now, the focus will be on how to adequately integrate materials into the cooperative work group experience.

The most critical decision required of the teacher entails the specific research goals for the students, which, in turn, impacts what research materials to acquire. All too often these materials are not strongly considered, resulting in a less-than-satisfying group experience. The basic guidelines for choosing materials for the teacher to follow include the following:

- Is the *primary* learning goal for the project to have the students *work with the information* contained within the material?

- Is the *primary* learning goal for the project to have the students *learn how to conduct research?*

These are not simplistic questions, but rather fundamental variables tied to the success of the learning experience, especially at the elementary and middle school levels. Experience has demonstrated that for every hour a typical fourth grader spends in the school library media center, fifty-five minutes will most likely be spent on searching for materials and only five minutes on reading and working with the information that is ultimately located. Although this is a blanket generalization, most elementary school teachers would attest it is close to the truth.

In other words, the teacher initially needs to determine if the most important goal for the students during the cooperative group work experience is to learn a body of curricular material, or if the most important goal is to learn how to use specific research skills.

If the teacher's primary goal is for the students to learn a body of curricular material, then the energy must be directed to physically providing as much research material as possible. In this fashion the student optimally spends only five minutes searching for information, and fifty-five minutes actually working with the data. This can be easily accomplished in a number of ways:

• Check out books, periodicals, and reference materials ahead of time from a library resource center, with pertinent sections selected and bookmarked for the students.

• Identify specific URLs for the students to investigate, rather than have them use search engines and directories to locate Internet sites.

• Create a vertical file system, especially if a teacher plans on incorporating cooperative work group experiences into the curricula on a permanent, year-to-year basis.

A vertical file system involves the creation of file folders divided into different topics, with each one containing varying bits of information for the students to use in their research. These materials may include reproductions of individual pages of books and encyclopedias, pages printed off of the Internet, or various types of supplementary materials acquired by the teacher.[1] The teacher highlights the pertinent sections on each of the pages, directing the student to this material.

For example, as part of the students' American History curriculum, a fifth-grade teacher plans to create a unit on pioneer life in the late 1800s. Integrated into that unit, the teacher plans a cooperative work group experience where the students investigate different features of life at that time on the Great Plains. Subsequently, vertical files might be compiled on the following relevant subjects, each of which is the primary topic area of one of the cooperative work groups:

• Frontier Culture and Social Life
• Food
• Organizing a Homestead
• Native Americans
• Lives of Children
• Transportation and Land Acquisition

Each file would contain pages labeled with specific, individual, subtopics. The material would be highlighted, keying the students directly to the relevant information. Using the example above, the file on "Organizing a Homestead" could typically contain individual pages and important information on the following topics:

• Farming Problems for Homesteaders
• Homesteader Food
• Homesteading Women
• How Homesteaders Started
• Pictures

- Solutions to Farming Problems
- Types of Housing, Add-Ons, Floors

Although most often used in the Social Sciences, the vertical file system can be applied to cooperative work group situations in all subjects. For example, a middle school science unit on Space Exploration might contain vertical files on the following topics:

- Planets
- Stars
- Other Extraterrestrial Objects: Comets, Meteors, Asteroids
- The History of Space Exploration
- Is There Life Outside of Our System?

As with the history example above, each of these files would contain pages labeled with specific, individual, subtopics. For example, the file titled The History of Space Exploration might contain specific curricular material on these topics:

- Before Sputnik
- The Mercury Project
- The Gemini Project
- The Apollo Project
- Space Stations—Past, Present, and Future
- The Space Shuttle
- The Russian Space Program
- The Future

By using this type of system the groups *immediately* receive and work with the information and materials they require for a successful cooperative work group activity, without using valuable time searching for the data. "Work time," therefore, becomes significantly more efficient for the students. The teacher, by controlling the various types of materials the students will use, ensures that the students will be exposed to the best curricular resources—versus relying on the students to ultimately locate their important information during their individual investigations. "Research skills" are taught and practiced during a lesson where the primary goal is learning "how to do research," versus spending the time in a content-based lesson such as this.

Creating vertical files is time-consuming. Consequently, it is important for the teacher to remember that the educational materials in the folders can be used repeatedly year after year. To extend the life of the material, the pages can be laminated or simply reproduced as they become worn.

Ultimately, the most efficient solution would be for the entire school staff to buy into a vertical file system. This would greatly reduce the workload for any one teacher. By having a vertical file system accessible to all teachers, everyone can contribute to it as they develop units throughout the year. This type of curricular cooperation works well across grade levels. Annually, the various curricular topic areas can be divided equally among the teachers. Subsequently, each teacher will research and create vertical files for one or two units. Teachers can then share the supplemental materials without having to recreate their own. Teachers hesitant about sharing their personal collections can have the pages reproduced for the vertical files, thereby allowing access to all. Everyone's workload is ultimately reduced, and the amount of research material available for the cooperative work groups is significantly increased.

PUTTING THEORY INTO PRACTICE: COLLECTING CURRICULAR MATERIAL FOR STUDENT USE

Mr. Washington had a dilemma as he was planning his cooperative work group experience. The project did not involve specific curricular material, nor did it entail an area of the curriculum covered by traditional, classroom materials. Since he also had a time constraint, he did not want his students to waste time unnecessarily in an attempt to locate information. Ultimately, he reviewed his perceived notions of the potential areas in which each group would operate, and created vertical files to help guide the students, when appropriate, in their research. Some groups were provided only with Internet addresses (URLs) to use. Others were given more extensive information. The following are the basic contents of these various files:

Drama Group

• The URL for the metasearch engine METACRAWLER,[2] which would enable the students to locate appropriate and useful Internet sites through searching under key words such as "homeless" and "hungry."

• The URL of the Internet site 54 WAYS TO HELP THE HOMELESS, a complete reproduction of the book by the same name.

• A brochure published by the county human services division, listing the various local support agencies and their contact numbers.

Music Group

• All of the material included in the Drama Group file, mentioned above.

• Copies of material located online by members of the Drama Group.

• A cassette tape of the song "God Help the Outcasts" (Menken & Schwartz, 1996).

Literature Group

• All of the material included in the Drama Group file, mentioned above.

• Copies of material located online by members of the Drama Group.

• A videocassette of the Comic Relief anecdotes originally presented to the whole class at the beginning of the project.

Brochure Group (Investigation)

• All of the material included in the Drama Group file, mentioned above.

• Copies of material located online by members of the Drama Group.

• Copies of the telephone directory pages that list the various human services organizations within their community.

• Brochures and information published by community help agencies and accumulated by Mr. Washington.

• The URL for the Internet site VOLUNTEER MATCH, which located various active service projects in their geographical area.

Brochure Group (Publication)

• No informational vertical file was provided for this group. Rather, they shared the material that the Brochure Group (Investigation) produced as it was compiled and completed throughout the project.

With these basic informational resources directly available in the form of vertical files, Mr. Washington believed that his students could immediately begin their project using the data, rather than spend valuable, and limited, classroom time researching information.

NOTES

1. Be sure to review the acceptable use policy followed by your state and district as it pertains to the reproduction and educational use of copyrighted material.

2. These Internet terms and sites are discussed in full in Part III. As stated earlier, all URLs are included in Resource A.

Teacher Role

Critical Thinking and Classroom Management

5

CRITICAL THINKING: A CORE COMPONENT OF STUDENT WORK

Much of the earlier writings on cooperative group work either state, or imply, that the role of teachers is to serve as a facilitator in the students' learning; that their role is transformed into one of secondary suppliers of information, rather than the primary role prevalent in traditional frontal teaching methodologies (Slavin, 1995). In addition, these writings also state, or imply, that students will automatically exhibit higher levels of critical thinking skills through the use of cooperative groups, simply because of the structure of the student interactions.

Subsequent research on cooperative group work shows this to be far from the truth (Mandel, 1991). Contrary to these beliefs, it has been demonstrated that the teacher is *directly* responsible for the critical thinking levels of the students in cooperative groups. In the aforementioned study on cooperative learning (see Chapter 3, Leadership), one of the variables analyzed was how the critical thinking level of the teacher's questioning affected the level of the students' subsequent critical thinking, as observed within group discussions.

The results of this study were enlightening and disturbing. In *every* instance throughout the year, in *every* cooperative learning situation, the students worked at the level of the teacher's final questions or statements to the students. In other words, the last teacher statement or question to the group determined the subsequent critical thinking level of the students. This occurred whether the teacher was talking to the entire class, to one particular group, or to an individual student. Figure 5.1 is an actual example from the study, with the "thinking level" based on Bloom's Taxonomy (Bloom, 1953):

The repercussions of this phenomenon are highly significant. Teachers conducting cooperative work group experiences are not simply facilitators. Rather, they are directly responsible for the level of a student's critical thinking. Teachers must therefore be actively involved in all phases of the learning process, taking particular notice of their interactions with the students. This is especially important in the area of teacher questioning.

Figure 5.1   Critical Thinking Levels During Teacher/Group Interaction Periods

Task Area	Thinking Level	Examples
Initial discussion	Teacher: Knowledge	T: What do you need to know about getting food?
	Student: Knowledge	S: How they did it. And what materials they used to do it?
Directing next data collection	T: Comprehension	T: Are you looking for the questions or the answers first? [Leaves group]
	S: Comprehension	S: We have to make up our own questions and then we have to answer them ourselves . . . Like what the farmers used for farming? Now I get it . . . We're not supposed to answer them yet. These are just questions we're writing down so we can get an idea.
Checking on data collection	T: Analysis	T: Look at the topics and see if you want your topics to overlap each other, or do you want your topics to be totally separate. Look at what you have so far.
	S: Analysis	[Discussion pros/cons of overlapping] We'll look up different things . . . One of us could look up equipment. We could look up things they used for cooking, one for finding food . . .
Evaluating work & decisions	T: Evaluation & analysis[1]	T: Try fitting all your questions into those categories. Rearrange your questions and see if it works. [Leaves group]
	S: Evaluation & analysis	S: What shall we put in "cooking"? Would "cooking" and "cooking equipment" be together? . . . Now we're going to put what they used for cooking into that section . . . [Group continues to analyze topics and questions]

NOTE: 1. Although categorizing questions would normally be considered by many to involve comprehension critical thinking skills, two of the analysts for these data believed the students incorporated analysis thinking skills. This belief was based on their position that the students did not have any previous direction on the makeup of the overall question categories that they eventually developed.

SOURCE: Mandel, 1991, pp. 134–136

CLASSROOM MANAGEMENT

One of the primary concerns of teachers new to the cooperative learning methodology has always been the use of successful classroom management skills, especially in handling problems between students. The importance of good classroom management cannot be understated. Effective classroom management can lead directly to the wonderful success of a cooperative work group experience, during the project and throughout the remainder of the year. Ineffective classroom management may result in chaos.

Successful and productive cooperative working groups are not the only positive outcome of good classroom management. As was discussed in the first chapter, learning how to work with and get along with others is the primary concern of today's employers. Unfortunately, it is also a basic skill that traditional classrooms often do not provide. Although "working in groups" is a normal occurrence socially on the playground, or within informal education situations, students need to be taught how to work successfully in groups in a more formalized academic setting. This is basic for their future success in adult work experiences. A teacher's classroom management techniques within cooperative work group methodology is now a primary resource for students to attain these crucial work-related skills.

The most important, and probably the hardest, classroom management skill for the teacher to exhibit to cooperative work groups is to learn *how to ignore situations*, or how *not to react* to problems unless the entire class is disrupted. This is especially true when responding to problems within individual groups. Minor disputes need to be resolved by the members involved, for social development is a supplemental goal of all cooperative work groups. One of the most basic and fundamental tenets of the cooperative work group concept is that the student members need to be accountable to one another as they develop their interpersonal relationship roles within the group.

One of the most important, and most frequent, times for the teacher *not* to get involved is when the group is not working. In an extended cooperative work group experience, a group "not working" one day is not a critical issue. Over the course of the project there will usually be time to catch up on their tasks. When it extends for a long period, they will learn that if they do not work, their task does not get accomplished, and negative repercussions ultimately result. These negative repercussions may range from receiving a lower grade on the final project, to having to spend additional time outside of the class completing their group work, to facing negative reactions from peers who were depending on the noninvolved students' material.

Self-motivation is a critical skill for success, in secondary and post-secondary education as well as in the general adult work place. Students need to internalize that completing a task is the correct thing to do—intrinsic motivation—rather than a result of the teacher's intervention—external motivation.

If given an adequate opportunity, most groups will resolve their own problems. However, teachers need to be cognizant of the fact that precedent is surprisingly strong within classrooms. As soon as a teacher begins to solve problems for the students, the tendency will be for them to "sit back" and let the teacher solve their problems, for it is an easier alternative than solving the problems themselves.

The same is true for groups that come to the teacher for answers or for curricular information during their research time. If the teacher provides answers or information in situations where the students could do it on their own, it is interpreted by the students as, "Why should I figure this out on my own when the teacher will do it for me?"

This does not mean that assistance should never be provided. Under various conditions, it should be readily given. However, just as teachers need to pick and choose when to intervene during problem situations, they also need to be selective as to when to help working groups.

For example, when students request assistance during their group work time, the teacher needs to decide which of the following scenarios is in operation:

• Is the information or material requested something that the students could locate with a little extra effort? If yes, then the teacher should not provide assistance and should allow the group to solve its informational problem.

• Is the information or material request involving an area not initially foreseen, such as a curricular direction not anticipated by the teacher? Then assistance should be given to the students, including how to locate the required material quickly and efficiently.

• If the information or material requested is something that was unclear in the teacher's directions, then clarification should be offered.

Probably the most helpful tool for the teacher to use in solving problems is the incorporation of a debriefing session at the end of every cooperative work group period. A debriefing session normally takes from five to ten minutes, depending on the tasks and problems of the groups. In the debriefing, the students freely share concerns and problems and offer each other valuable solutions. Debriefing also allows the students to share information relevant to their group tasks, or to help their peers locate required data.

Some of the things that may occur during a debriefing session include the following:

• Groups can share resolutions to problems that they have experienced, be they interpersonal, such as an uncooperative member, or a curricular problem, such as difficulty in locating materials or fulfilling a particular group task.

• Students can offer solutions to those groups with problems, based on their own group experience or by sharing personal knowledge of materials or direction in areas requested by other groups.

• The teacher can do a quick formative evaluation of the progress of the groups and the status of the learning experience. Questions can be asked and information shared and evaluated.

• An overview and discussion of the next step of the learning experience makes each group aware of what is expected between class sessions and during the subsequent work period. The next work group session may begin much quicker and work more efficiently.

Overall, the information shared in a debriefing session can alleviate many of the classroom management problems experienced by the teacher. This procedure provides the students with opportunities to take ownership of their difficulties, and also to receive peer feedback for possible solutions.

PUTTING THEORY INTO PRACTICE: PLANNING FOR HIGHER-ORDER THINKING SKILLS AND DEALING WITH PROBLEMS

Mr. Washington was aware of the research pertaining to the role of teachers in cooperative group work situations, and he always attempted to word his statements and questions using higher-level critical thinking verbiage; he knew that "on the spot," it was much more difficult. Consequently, he prepared questions ahead of time that he used throughout the project that addressed the higher critical thinking skills. Some were developed before the students began their investigation; some were developed as a result of their experiences.

The following is a partial list of some of the higher-order critical thinking questions that Mr. Washington used throughout the students' work time:

• How can you get the audience to make an emotional connection with the plight of the homeless through your scene/song/brochure?

• What are the most important points that you want the audience to learn about the homeless? Why are they so important?

• What are the least important points for the audience to learn? (Keep in mind time constraints for the presentation, space constraints for the brochure, and attention-span/interest constraints for this particular audience). Why are these not important?

• How have you covered the important points in your scene/song/brochure?

• Is the information adequately distributed throughout the drama, music, and brochure presentations, or is there too much repetition?

• Are there additional places that you can contact/research to provide more information?

• Is there a more creative approach or format to present some of your material and information?

• Have you compared your material with that of other groups to share information and avoid duplication?

These are some of the questions that Mr. Washington asked throughout the cooperative work group experience to have the students work at a higher critical thinking level on all stages of their project.

Classroom management issues had to be dealt with on the very first day of Washington's project. The Literature Group was having difficulties that prevented them from completing any work. The group was initially upset that Sean was assigned to their team for he had poor grades and work habits. The other members did not want their personal grades potentially lowered because of his lack of academic performance.

Within twenty minutes of the group work time, a few of the members of the Literature Group came to Mr. Washington complaining that Sean was disruptive and not doing any work. Without further comment, Mr. Washington simply answered the students, "Work it out among yourselves."

Within the next ten minutes, members came to him two more times. Again, he repeated the same response.

Although the students were obviously getting very little work done, he knew that the project would last for at least a week, and that there would be sufficient opportunity for the group to make up this time.

During the debriefing session, Mr. Washington asked if any group was having difficulty with the project. Immediately, Ashley raised her hand to complain about Sean and his lack of cooperation. Rather than admonishing Sean—a reaction that everyone expected—Mr. Washington asked him if it was true, to which Sean responded, "Yes." When Mr. Washington asked why he was uncooperative, Sean said, "Because they gave me _____ to do, which I didn't want to do."

Mr. Washington then turned to Ashley and inquired, "Is this true?"

Ashley answered, "Yes. We all picked the jobs we wanted, and that one was left."

Mr. Washington then summarized, "So, you all picked the jobs you wanted, and the one that no one wanted, you gave to Sean. Correct?"

Ashley hesitantly answered, "Yes."

Smiling at Sean, Mr. Washington replied, "Well, under those conditions, if I were Sean, I would have probably been uncooperative too." Then, turning to the rest of the class, he asked, "Did any other groups have difficulty dividing up the tasks?" A couple of groups raised their hands. "How did you solve your problem?" At that point the various groups shared their experiences, after which Mr. Washington said to the Literature Group, "Tomorrow, why don't you try one of those solutions?"

The following day, Mr. Washington quietly noticed that the Literature Group was working very smoothly, and that there were no complaints about Sean, who was working quite well. During the debriefing session, he questioned the Literature Group about whether or not their previous problem had been resolved. Ashley answered that it had. He then inquired as to how Sean was working that day. She replied, "Sean was great! We gave him _____ to do, and he was working on it the whole period." Mr. Washington then turned to Sean and asked him if things had worked out, and he too responded that he was happy today. The tasks, in his perspective, had been distributed fairly, and he now felt he was a full member of the group.

The Literature Group operated smoothly until it suffered a major setback. During that particular work session, Sean was absent. He had become such an integral part of the group that the group had problems functioning without him!

During the cooperative work group project, the important aspects of classroom management that Mr. Washington experienced included the following:

- Allowing a group to solve their own problem, rather than solving it for them.

- Allowing other groups to share similar experiences and their solutions, permitting peer learning to occur.

- Allowing the opportunity to raise the self-esteem of a student who normally had difficulty succeeding in any academic area, and who was considered, by his peers, a group liability.

Assessment 6

Formal assessment of cooperative work groups is one of the greatest concerns of students and their parents, especially in secondary schools. Students are fearful that their marks might be adversely affected by circumstances beyond their control—such as their nonworking group partners. This is particularly the case when one is working with above-average achieving students.

Unfortunately, there is not an overall rule for assessment of cooperative work group experiences. There is no methodology relevant and successful for all cooperative work group situations. There are too many variables involved, ranging from dealing with different curricula, to using different types of goals for each experience. As stated earlier, the goal of some lessons is to learn specific curricular material, the goal of some lessons is to learn supplemental or varying material on a topic, and the goal of some other lessons may be to address a classroom social issue or problem. There is no single assessment method that would be appropriate for use in each situation. There are, however, some underlying principles that the teacher can follow in order to alleviate student, and parent, concerns. These include the following:

Matching the Assessment to the Goals

The teacher must initially address what is being assessed. This seemingly simplistic step is often overlooked. Before any assessment is planned or created, teachers need to refer to the established goals for this experience; once again, goals that have been derived from your state's or district's educational standards.

The introductory question to be asked is whether or not the cooperative group experience is the major part of the overall curricular unit, or simply a supplemental section? If the group work sessions are where the majority of the curricular information is to be obtained by the students, then some form of formal assessment is required to ascertain whether or not they have acquired that specific knowledge. The subsequent form taken by that assessment is wholly dependent on the material, subject matter, age of the students, and the classroom learning environment. There is no one form or structure of assessment that is relevant and applicable to every learning situation, subject matter, or age group.

What is to be assessed relates directly to how the group experience was formulated, and how the required materials and resources were provided. If each group was to acquire specific curricular knowledge that is to be assessed, then the *opportunity* for each group to attain that knowledge must have been provided.

Conversely, if the group learning experience was supplementary to the overall unit, then a formal written assessment may not be necessary, or valid, for many students will have learned material that others did not. Rather, the group's report of their findings may be a sufficient way of determining whether or not the project was a worthwhile curricular event, and that student learning occurred.

Either way, the assessment must be designed to demonstrate to the teacher whether or not the goals of the specific learning experience have been met. This can be done only if the cooperative work group learning experience is viewed holistically within the overall curricular unit.

Assessment should also be conducted *informally* throughout the cooperative work group experience. This type of formative evaluation can provide the teacher relevant data to use in adjusting the learning experience, or altering it in the future.[1]

Teachers can informally interview students both throughout the cooperative work group sessions and at the end of the project, asking them variations of three basic questions:

- What has the student learned in the experience?

- What did/does the experience mean for the student? (How does it affect the student cognitively and affectively?)

- What will the student remember in the future about the experience and the content that was covered?

Anecdotal evidence collected throughout the cooperative work group experience can also contribute to the overall assessment of the project. An experienced teacher can qualitatively "sense" how a cooperative work group session is going. This type of "educational connoisseurship" (Eisner, 1994) is an important and valid tool to use when assessing the overall quality of the program.

Being Fair

Above all, the teacher must be fair. This statement is not quite as simplistic as it sounds. For example, take the use of "group grades," a common form of assessment with cooperative learning. Group grades are when one specific mark is given to all members of the same group, regardless of their individual contributions. However, if a group grade is given on a project, and the teacher knows that certain students did work above and beyond—or significantly less than—the work performed by the rest of the group, then individual marks should be adjusted. That is what is meant by "fairness." The grades should accurately reflect the individual's work and effort. This adjusted group grade procedure can easily be determined in a number of ways:

Teacher observations. As the groups are working over the length of the unit, the teacher takes note of who is continuously on-task, and who is not. Anecdotal evidence is to be maintained by the teacher, if it appears as if an adjusted group grade may be necessary.

Information From the Debriefing Sessions. Often information will be provided during the debriefing sessions as to who has done extraordinary work, and who has been problematic to the group process. Again, anecdotal evidence must be recorded.

Ask the Students. Question the students within the group as to who did what work. In front of peers, students are frightfully honest as to their individual contributions.

Figure 6.1   A Typical Adjusted Group Grade Assessment

Student	Work That the Individual Students Did Within the Group Project	Adjusted Group Grade
1	Adequately researched the section of the project assigned within the group and wrote a report (e.g., 3–4 pages) Also personally created a multimedia poster illustrating the material.	A-
2	Adequately researched the section of the project assigned within the group and wrote a report (e.g., 3–4 pages)	B
3	Adequately researched the section of the project assigned within the group and wrote a report (e.g., 3–4 pages)	B
4	Adequately researched the section of the project assigned within the group and wrote a report (e.g., 3–4 pages)	B
5	Did about half of the research the others accomplished (e.g., 1–1/2 pages)	C

Using the adjusted group grade assessment process is quite easy, especially once the teacher really has gotten to know the work habits, work levels, and personalities of the individual students. Figure 6.1 contains a very basic example of this procedure, using a typical group project presentation as the basis for the grade. In this scenario, the overall group grade was a "B." However, the teacher determined that at least one student did significantly more work than the other group members, and one did much less work. Hence the adjusted group grade. (Please note that this rubric is simplistic and "generic." The actual variables graded within the working rubric would be determined through the goals of the teacher for that particular project. In an actual classroom rubric, the categories would have greater detail, specifics, and benchmark examples.)

Students, and ultimately parents, accept the adjusted group grade process once they understand how it operates, and how it is meant to make a cooperative work group grade "fair" and "valid." This can be accomplished very simply. Early in the cooperative work group experience the teacher needs to explain the expectations; provide the students (and often the parents) with a copy of the rubrics, along with benchmark examples; and ask them for feedback. Once the students know the expectations, and that they will not be unfairly penalized for the underachievement of any group members, dissatisfaction with the group grading process is greatly reduced. When questions do arise, objective evidence is provided to support—or alter—the teacher's decision. This evidence can be either student product or anecdotal descriptions of behavior, as noted by the teacher.

Being Able to Justify One's Decisions

Above all, whenever any form of group grade is provided, the teacher should role-play a situation in which a disgruntled parent is questioning the assessment. If the mark can be objectively justified through work examples, or anecdotally with examples of student work and behavior during the cooperative work group experience, then the teacher's grade is justified. However, if the teacher cannot adequately support the mark, then a reevaluation should be conducted, using the previous two principles of assessment.

Formal assessment is a major component in any educational experience, especially in today's society, where the value of teaching too often is tied to a standardized test. In light of this, nontraditional educational experiences—such as cooperative work group activities—need to be "assessed" in some fashion that is palatable to all stake holders: parents, students, the community, and administrators.

If the principles of matching the assessment to the goals, being fair, and being able to justify one's decisions are followed, then assessment can become a nonproblematic experience and can truly inform the teacher, the students, the administrators, and the parents as to value of the cooperative work group learning experience as a valid and productive educational option.

PUTTING THEORY INTO PRACTICE: ASSESSING THE EXPERIENCE

In his cooperative work group experience, Mr. Washington initially determined that the learning experience was not tied to specific curriculum, thus the assessment that he selected would be more subjective. He also decided to focus his assessment on a limited number of key areas, each with its own particular and appropriate format. The three areas that he selected included the following:

- The effectiveness of the designed learning experience
- The effort and product of the students within their group work
- The effectiveness of the group presentation

For the first area, the effectiveness of the learning experience as designed, Mr. Washington did his own personal assessment in his mind, using his extensive teaching repertoire that he had acquired over many years of teaching. Throughout the cooperative work group experience he made note of the following:

- Were the students on-task throughout the process?
- Were there unexpected problems with the materials, the task, or group dynamics?
- Did the students use higher-order critical thinking skills throughout their discussions and work?
- Did the students "enjoy" and appreciate the experience?
- How could the learning experience be improved for the following year?

For his second assessment area, to determine the effort and product of the students within their group work, Mr. Washington developed a rubric for each of the groups, based on the particular tasks of the group. Since the product of each group was different from the others, he had to make a separate rubric for each of them. However, because he had conducted similar cooperative work group experiences in the past, he was able to use some from previous projects, rather than create new ones. Figure 6.2 is an example of the rubric that he used for the Drama Group.

Although there was no formal, written assessment applicable for this production, Mr. Washington was able to determine each student's participation through the use of three different methods:

Figure 6.2   Mr. Washington's Rubric for the Drama Group

Grade	Requirements
A	Participates fully in the informational research, the writing of the scene, and either acting or being part of the production staff of the presentation
B	Participates fully in two of the following three facets: the informational research, the writing of the scene, and either acting or being part of the production staff of the presentation
C	Participates fully in one of the following three facets: the informational research, the writing of the scene, and either acting or being part of the production staff of the presentation
D	Shows minimal participation in the informational research, the writing of the scene, and either acting or being part of the production staff of the presentation
F	Refuses to participate in any aspect of the informational research, the writing of the scene, and the production of the final presentation

- His personal observation of the students throughout the cooperative work group experience

- The personal assessment written by each student of his or her involvement in the various facets of the project

- The informal individual interviews with the students within the group in which the students evaluated each other's contribution to each section

For the last assessment area, Mr. Washington studied the effectiveness of the group presentation in three ways:

- The reactions (positive and negative) to the presentations by the audience

- Informal conversations with a limited number of his teaching peers as to how other students reacted to the presentation and brochure—both positively and negatively

- A survey his students developed at a later date that was given randomly to a few classes to determine any changes in their behavior and attitudes toward the homeless

Through these three types of formal and informal assessment techniques, Mr. Washington was able to ascertain whether or not his original goals were met during the cooperative work group experience, and the types of changes or modifications to be implemented if he chose to replicate the program the following year.

A FINAL NOTE

The formulation and operation of the student groups is but one component of the successful cooperative work group experience, albeit probably the most important

Figure 6.3   Summary of the Five Variables of Cooperative Work Groups

Five Variables Of Cooperative Work Groups

1. *Group Formation*

   • Ideal size: 4–6 (3 leads to social decisions; 7 is a committee)
   • Heterogeneous/homogenous, depending on goals
   • Variables to be addressed: readers vs. nonreaders, special education students, English language learners, and access to the Internet (school vs. home)

2. *Leadership*

   • A personality trait—to be determined by the group
   • Provide tasks, leadership determines distribution

3. *Materials*

   • Must have enough!
   • Focus of the lesson—research skills vs. using the curricular material?
   • Use vertical files/Internet

4. *Teacher Role: Critical Thinking and Classroom Management*

   • An active facilitator
   • Maintains/implements use of high critical thinking levels
   • Let the groups do problem solving, not the teacher
   • Debriefing

5. Assessment

   • Matching the assessment to the goals
   • Being fair
   • Being able to justify one's decisions

one. However, to truly achieve curricular success in this area, teachers need to be cognizant of the numerous important characteristics of the process:

• Group formation
• Student leadership variable
• Acquiring sufficient materials
• The teacher role: students' critical thinking and how to deal with classroom management issues
• How best to conduct an assessment of the learning experience

Once this is accomplished, the other two components of the cooperative work group experience can be addressed: how to increase student learning and achievement through the identification of how individual students best learn (the multiple intelligences), and how to obtain access to an "endless" supply of curricular material via online educational resources (the Internet).

NOTE

1. See Henerson, Morris, and Fitz-Gibbon (1978) for a detailed discussion on how to conduct this type of "informal" assessment.

Part II

The Way Students Learn Effectively and Efficiently

PUTTING THEORY INTO PRACTICE: WHY DO THEY ALL HAVE TO BE SO DIFFERENT?

As Mr. Washington observed his cooperative work groups on the homeless, he noticed problems concerning the work habits and product of different students, none of which would preclude their groups from functioning well. But still, it was enough for him to harbor some concerns relating to the personal success of the individuals. Two students in particular stood out in his mind, Sean and Sally.

Sean, who was intelligent and designated "gifted," rarely turned in all of his work. Those written assignments submitted were almost always short and concise. The work he did eventually inevitably turn in was consistently correct, even when the answers provided were the bare minimum. Even without completing a significant portion of his work, Sean managed to pass every test with an "A."

In the cooperative group work experience, Sean, who was assigned to the Literature Group, rarely did much written work, and what he did complete, was minimal. For example, when he was asked to report on the operating information for the Mid-City Food Bank, he submitted the following:

M-F

6–6

(XXX) XXX-XXXX

Call 1st

Annette Johnson—Director

Although he had submitted all of the pertinent information concerning the food bank, it was not in a format usable for the brochure without considerable additions. Nor did he provide any extra information that might be helpful to the reader. However, when his group questioned him about the city food bank, he was able to provide them with a full description of the organization, including the function of the charity and their rules and policies. Sean was also completely involved in all of the group's discussions, often being the source of ideas on locating important project information.

Mr. Washington concluded that Sean was a student with a lot of academic potential, after reviewing his written papers and observing his work habits within and outside the cooperative work group. However, Sean was very lazy, and attempted to do only the minimum amount of work allowable without significant penalty (e.g., a negative parent conference or an overall grade lower than a "B").

Sally presented a totally different situation. She was assigned to the Music Group because of a high musical multiple intelligence. She was also an excellent student in all of her academic subjects. Within her group, she wrote many of the song lyrics that this group produced. Yet, she was driving Mr. Washington crazy.

Every time Mr. Washington gave a direction to the class or to her group, she inevitably approached him for additional explanation, which she would continue to do until she was satisfied. Whenever instructed to "figure it out on her own," she became frustrated and would not function until she was given the additional direction, either by one of her friends, or most often, by Mr. Washington. Once she thoroughly understood what was being asked of her, she completed the task at a very high, successful level.

Upon reflection, Mr. Washington considered Sally to be immature, but an excellent student. He felt she was both unable to figure things out for herself, and craved the teacher's attention.

Mr. Washington was completely perplexed by both of these students. None of his traditional teaching and classroom management strategies seemed to work with these two particular students. These behaviors were not correlated with the cooperative work group assignment, and had been evidenced throughout the year regardless of the subject matter, classroom organization, or teaching methodology. Sean rarely turned in written work. When he did, it was the bare minimum. Sally needed a personal explanation for every assignment she was given.

Mr. Washington consulted his analysis of the multiple intelligences test that he had given to the students at the beginning of the year. He had previously studied the data when formulating the project cooperative work groups. At that time, however, he was concentrating only on those students with the appropriate intelligences for their groups, such as bodily-kinesthetic for those in the Drama Group, Musical for those in the Music Group, linguistic for those in the Literature Group, logical-mathematical for those in the Brochure (Investigation) Group, and spatial for those in the Brochure (Publication) Group. He took only limited notice of the other intelligences.

To his surprise, Mr. Washington noticed the following high and low multiple intelligences scores for Sean and Sally. The scores were rated on a scale of zero to five, "zero" representing virtually no aptitude for components of that intelligence, "five" representing an extremely high aptitude for that area:

Sean:

Linguistic score: 0

Logical-mathematical score: 5

Sally:

Linguistic score:	4
Logical-mathematical score:	5
Spatial score:	1

The scores immediately explained the behavior of the two students to Mr. Washington.

Sean, according to the multiple intelligences test, had little to no aptitude for expressing himself linguistically or for using written language. However, he was extremely logical. Thus in the classroom, because he was so uncomfortable with using language, he would do the absolute minimum on any written assignments. His particular strength, to understand the logical organization of the curricular material and to extract the important components to use and to study for any assignments, resulting in his high test scores even though he completed little of the required written work.

This learning behavior was reflected strongly in the cooperative work group experience where Sean used a minimum number of words in his submitted work, but when questioned directly, provided detailed information about the place he investigated.

As a result of this new analysis, Mr. Washington lowered his expectations for Sean's *quantity* of written work but expected a high quality and completeness of all assignments.

Mr. Washington now realized that Sally's logical-mathematical intelligence was her overriding strength. Her scores indicated that she cognitively needed to see the "logic" of any work activity in which she participated. In order to function at her optimum level, it was essential all of the steps were sequentially "spelled out." Once the required, specific procedures were internalized, she had no problem with completing her task on an overall high-quality level.

As a result of this new analysis, Mr. Washington immediately became more patient with Sally, allowing her to request additional explanations throughout each cooperative work group session. In fact, whenever absent, Mr. Washington would note in his lesson plans for the substitute that Sally would continually request information concerning the assigned learning activity, and that the substitute should be patient with her.

By understanding and evaluating the individual strengths and weaknesses of his students' multiple intelligences, Mr. Washington was able to tailor the classroom learning environment and his teaching behaviors to the students' special and specific needs. As a result, he maximized the learning potential of individual students, making their experience more positive, productive, and ultimately, more efficient.

Brain Research

The Multiple Intelligences

7

A QUICK OVERVIEW

One of the three components of the cooperative work group concept is to discover the most efficient and effective way for the students to learn on an individual basis. Rather than solely concentrate on the classroom "whole," the cooperative work group concept borrows from current business world thought by focusing on improving the chances for each individual to reach his or her potential. This is an important component of successful adult work groups (see Beebe & Masterson, 1999; Hackman, 2002; Hackman et al., 1983). For this reason, a thorough examination of the topic is appropriate, with a special emphasis on how teachers can integrate the theory into their classroom environment.

Toward the end of the twentieth century, brain research became a very popular area in educational research, and gradually grew into an important aspect of discovering how children best learn. Its importance has reached the point where the theory is regularly incorporated into the inservice work conducted by most educational institutions. Whereas there are numerous studies and theories on how students learn—too numerous to summarize in this work[1]—Howard Gardner's theory of the multiple intelligences (1993, 1999) has proven to be one of the most popular and helpful tools for the classroom teacher. Its popularity and applicability to the classroom has led to its direct integration into the cooperative work group concept.[2]

Gardner's theory derived from the desire to go beyond the standard "IQ" score. He maintained that our culture defined "intelligence" too narrowly. In his view, intelligence was not something that could be determined from isolated tasks never done before, as those required in various components of a typical I.Q. test. Rather, he strongly believed that intelligence had more to do with one's "capacity for (1) solving problems and (2) fashioning products in a context-rich and naturalistic setting" (Armstrong, 2000, p. 1).

Howard Gardner proposed that everyone possesses, to some extent, eight basic intelligences.[3] Every individual has varying strengths and weaknesses within these eight intelligences. The following is a brief description of each of the intelligences as presented by Thomas Armstrong (2000), one of the leading researchers in the application of the multiple intelligences to the everyday classroom:

Linguistic Intelligence. The capacity to use words effectively, whether orally or in writing. This intelligence includes the ability to manipulate the syntax or structure of

Box 7.1

How Were the Eight Multiple Intelligences Determined?

The multiple intelligences were not simply "created" by Howard Gardner. An area became an "intelligence" only when it met several very specific, objective criteria. These are:

Potential Isolation by Brain Damage

Each intelligence is located in one specific part of the brain. People with brain damage in that area showed limited or no ability in that intelligence.

The Existence of Savants, Prodigies, and Other Exceptional Individuals

There are individuals who operate at an extremely high level in one particular intelligence, even though they may be extremely low in others.

A Distinctive Developmental History and a Definable Set of Expert "End-State" Performances

The intelligence shows a development pattern and a set end-state within some point in human development.

An Evolutionary History and Evolutionary Plausibility

Each intelligence is embedded within human evolution, and also is displayed in other species.

Support From Psychometric Findings

Many existing standardized tests provide support for each of the various intelligences.

language, the phonology or sounds of language, the semantics or meanings of language, and the pragmatic dimensions or practical uses of language.

Logical-Mathematical Intelligence. The capacity to use numbers effectively and to reason well. This intelligence includes sensitivity to logical patterns and relationships, statements and propositions, functions, and other related abstractions. The kinds of processes used in the service of logical-mathematical intelligence include categorization, classification, inference, generalization, calculation, and hypothesis testing.

Spatial Intelligence. The ability to perceive the visual-spatial world accurately and to perform transformations on those perceptions. This intelligence involves sensitivity to color, line, shape, form, space, and the relationships that exist among these elements. It includes the capacity to visualize, to graphically represent visual or spatial ideas, and to orient oneself appropriately in a spatial matrix.

Bodily-Kinesthetic Intelligence. Expertise in using one's whole body to express ideas and feelings and facility in using one's hands to produce or transform things. This intelligence includes specific physical skills such as coordination, balance, dexterity, strength, flexibility, and speed, as well as proprioceptive, tactile, and haptic capacities.

Musical Intelligence. The capacity to perceive, discriminate, transform, and express musical forms. This intelligence includes sensitivity to the rhythm, pitch or melody, and timbre or tone color of a musical piece. One can have a figural or "top down" understanding of music, a formal or "bottom-up" understanding, or both.

Interpersonal Intelligence. The ability to perceive and make distinctions in the moods, intentions, motivations, and feelings of other people. This can include sensitivity to facial expressions, voice, and gestures; the capacity for discriminating among many different kinds of interpersonal cues; and the ability to respond effectively to those cues in some pragmatic way.

Intrapersonal Intelligence. Self-knowledge and the ability to act adaptively on the basis of that knowledge. This intelligence includes having an accurate picture of oneself; awareness of inner moods, intentions, motivations, temperaments, and desires; and the capacity for self-discipline, self-understanding, and self-esteem.

Box 7.1 Continued

Support From Experimental Psychological Tasks

Certain psychological studies demonstrate intelligences working in isolation from each other.

An Identifiable Core Operative or Set of Operations

Each intelligence has specific sets of operations for that intelligence to function.

Susceptibility to Encoding in a Symbol System

Each intelligence has specific symbol systems that are associated with that area.

SOURCE: Adapted from Armstrong, 2000, pp. 3–8

Naturalist Intelligence. Expertise in the recognition and classification of the numerous species—the flora and fauna—of an individual's environment. This also includes sensitivity to other natural phenomena and, in the case of those growing up in an urban environment, the capacity to discriminate among nonliving forms such as cars, sneakers, and music CD covers. (Armstrong, 2000, see pp. 2–3)

INTEGRATING THE MULTIPLE INTELLIGENCES INTO THE CLASSROOM CURRICULUM

As stated above, there are many different opinions and philosophies concerning brain research. Even within multiple intelligence theory, there are a number of different opinions on what it means to the classroom, and how it should be implemented. A visit to any educational supply store provides numerous workbooks that guide the classroom teacher through the process. Some of them directly use the theory in a "pure" form; others adapt it in a way that the author deems appropriate. Whereas virtually all material concerning multiple intelligence theory refers to whole class experiences, most of it can be directly applied to cooperative work group experiences, during teacher-student and student-student interactions, and to individual work time.

The most significant problem with the theory is that it is not applicable or appropriate for every child or for every classroom situation. However, it *can* assist the teacher in helping students maximize their potential, and to understand—and

Box 7.2

When the Intelligences Cause You to Think Too Much . . .

I recently had the "unfortunate" opportunity of having a first-hand, personal experience with how strongly the multiple intelligences can operate within the human mind. My primary hobby has always been music, having grown up playing an instrument and singing, and having directed student vocal groups as an adult.

One night a few months ago, I attended a concert performed by the Los Angeles Philharmonic Orchestra at the Hollywood Bowl. Although the music being performed was written by one of my favorite composers, I soon discovered that I was experiencing tremendous difficulty in concentrating on the program. My mind continually drifted. I found that I could not stop thinking about various projects on which I was currently involved. As soon as I finished one thought, my attention went on to another. It soon became very frustrating as I felt I was missing an excellent concert.

Upon later reflection, I realized that my very high musical intelligence was the culprit. My seats at the Hollywood Bowl were far enough back from the orchestra that I ultimately received little visual stimulation from the orchestra (although the sound was incredible). Without any sensory activation but the music to which to attend, my mind was highly energized by the melodies. It provoked me to think. And think. And think. The result was I had difficulty "turning off" my cognition and simply relaxing and enjoying the music!

provide adaptations for—individual students. This is one of the goals of the cooperative work group concept.

The following pages provide one opinion on how to adapt multiple intelligences theory to the classroom, and ultimately, to all aspects of the cooperative work group concept.

The multiple intelligences provide the teacher with an idea of how students think, and the types of educational materials or presentation patterns that activate their cognitive abilities. This theory helps explain thinking patterns that have, in the past, been attributed to "personality quirks." For example, someone who seems to do his or her best thinking while jogging probably has a high bodily-kinesthetic intelligence. The physical action that is being undertaken activates the thinking process. Someone who works best while music is playing in the background would tend to have a high musical intelligence. One who needs to constantly talk out ideas with another person probably has a high interpersonal intelligence. Conversely, a person who requires time to reflect personally on ideas would tend to have a high intrapersonal intelligence. All of these examples are applicable to the student working as an individual part of a cooperative group project.

When incorporating the multiple intelligences into the curriculum, it is important to note that curricular materials do not have to be "presented" in that particular mode—that is, put algebraic equations into music; express a quadratic equation through body movements. This is a popular fallacy that hinders the use of the multiple intelligences. Some teachers do not see the practicality of presenting their material in "bodily-kinesthetic" or "musical," when that is not what the multiple intelligences theory promotes. Rather, these areas of intelligence are environmental or educational "conditions" that activate the mind. As such, they can be incorporated into the classroom environment and cooperative work group experience, regardless of the subject matter. Obviously, some curricular areas are harder to adapt with some of the intelligences than others (e.g., upper level math and science). But most of the multiple intelligences can be integrated into the classroom environment and curriculum in some form of presentation. See Box 7.3 for some examples, taken from both a history class and a science class.

CLASSROOM AND GROUP MANAGEMENT INCORPORATING THE MULTIPLE INTELLIGENCES

Multiple intelligence theory has numerous uses to the classroom teacher. The material above demonstrates how it can be integrated into the classroom environment and curriculum to activate student thinking. Much of this is directly applicable to the curricular aspects of cooperative work groups. However, one of the most important uses of the multiple intelligences theory is that it can help teachers look at potentially negative student behaviors in a completely new light. Behaviors that were once thought of as being disruptive, may actually be an active manifestation of that student's multiple intelligence level both in whole class and student group situations. Of course, this is *not* meant to be a blanket generalization—disruptive behaviors often have other underlying causes—but many of these student actions *may* be explained, and encouraged, through multiple intelligence theory.

Take the following scenarios into consideration. These are all classroom situations that regularly occur both in frontal teaching and in group work situations, and where a teacher may find a student's behavior disruptive:

Box 7.3

Examples of How to Integrate the Multiple Intelligences Into the Curriculum

- Someone with a high multiple intelligence in the linguistic area is cognitively activated through the use of words, be they written or oral.

  Example: Start a lesson on the Civil War with a verbal review of the material covered to date.

  Example: Start a lesson on chemical reactions with a verbal review of the material covered to date.

- Someone with a high multiple intelligence in the logical-mathematical area is cognitively activated through seeing the logical connections in the material.

  Example: Start a lesson on the Civil War with a flow chart on the board representing a cause/effect relationship of the events leading to today's lesson.

  Example: Start a lesson on chemical reactions by writing a sample chemical equation on the board and discussing how it relates to today's lesson.

- Someone with a high multiple intelligence in the spatial area is cognitively activated through visual representations of the material.

  Example: Start a lesson on the Civil War by displaying pictures from the period of the subject area to be covered.

  Example: Start a lesson on chemical reactions by displaying pictures of molecules combining into new compounds.

- Someone with a high multiple intelligence in the bodily-kinesthetic area is cognitively activated through some form of physical movement.

  Example: Begin a lesson on the Civil War with a student role-playing a person from the period who summarizes the previous lesson from the role-play character's point of view.

  Example: Start a lesson on chemical reactions with role-playing a scientist experimenting with the development of new compounds.

Box 7.3 Continued

• Someone with a high multiple intelligence in the musical area is cognitively activated through hearing some fashion of music.

   Example: Begin the lesson on the Civil War by playing period-related music as the students enter the room.

   Example: Start a lesson on chemical reactions with playing a short identifiable piece of music and discussing how the various parts (timbre, tone, melody) produce something new—similar to creating new compounds.

• Someone with a high multiple intelligence in the Interpersonal area is cognitively activated through interacting with someone else.

   Example: Start a lesson on the Civil War by pairing off students and having them review the material from the previous lesson.

   Example: Start a lesson on chemical reactions by pairing off students and having them review the material from the previous lesson.

• Someone with a high multiple intelligence in the Intrapersonal area is cognitively activated through personal reflection.

   Example: Have the students take the role of someone from the Civil War time period and, in character, write a reflective journal entry.

   Example: Start a lesson on chemical reactions by having the students individually hypothesize what would happen if they combined two compounds.

• Someone with a high multiple intelligence in the Naturalist area is cognitively activated through some form of interaction with nature.

   Example: Start a lesson on the Civil War by describing the natural setting of a place where the day's events could have occurred.

   Example: Start a lesson on chemical reactions by describing the combinations of elements and compounds in nature—for example, photosynthesis/acid rain.

A Student Is Constantly Doodling

Students who are constantly drawing or doodling during a lecture or discussion may have a high spatial intelligence. These students need to continuously work with some sort of visual representations to concentrate. Students with high spatial intelligence are thinking while drawing; they are on-task, as evidenced by their participation in the classroom discussion. Drawing allows them to concentrate and reflect on the material that is being presented. In a learning situation, students with a high spatial multiple intelligence who are not allowed to draw, but who are forced simply to sit quietly and attentively, may "turn-off" cognitively, or become truly off-task.

How does one deal with this type of student?

To deal effectively with these students, let them quietly draw or doodle, since this writing activates their thinking processes. If they do not take an active role in the classroom discussion, the teacher should occasionally ask these students questions to ensure that they are truly on-task. In a group situation, the other members of the group should actively include them in the discussions.

A Student Is Constantly Moving Around in the Seat, Tapping Something, or Fidgeting

Students who are constantly moving in their seats, tapping their pens, or fidgeting with some object, may very well have a high bodily-kinesthetic intelligence. Unfortunately, these students are most often diagnosed as either being ADHD (attention deficit disorder with hyperactivity), a discipline problem, or simply immature. Rather, they may need to have their body moving to activate their thinking processes. Students with a high bodily-kinesthetic intelligence who are not allowed to move but are forced to sit quietly and attentively, may "turn-off" cognitively, or become truly off-task.

How does one deal with this type of student?

These students need some kind of physical activity in order to focus cognitively. Therefore, a teacher should allow them to continue behaviors that are *not* disturbing anyone. An alternate solution is to provide, or let them bring in themselves, a quiet squeeze-type object that allows them to flex the muscles in their hands without disrupting anyone or being distracting. This also works in a group situation, along with allowing that student to be the group "gopher," the one who is designated to leave the group for materials and information.

A Student Is Constantly Trying to Work on Classroom Material With Someone Else

Students with a high interpersonal intelligence who constantly want to work with a partner are not necessarily trying to be social or attempting to copy someone else's work. Rather, they may very well be working solely on their own material. However, these students need to share ideas with another person, or need to have some personal contact in order to function cognitively. Students with high interpersonal intelligence who are not allowed to work in direct proximity with someone else, but are forced to sit quietly and do their own work in a solitary setting, may "turn-off" cognitively or go off-task.

How does one deal with this type of student?

The best way to deal with these students is to provide an opportunity for them to work with others. This can be directly accomplished in everyday class work through cooperative learning, letting two students sit quietly together using "twelve-inch voices,"[4] allowing pairs of students to work somewhere in the room where they will not disturb anyone else, or by moving the desks from isolated "rows" to small two- to four-person groups. The entire cooperative work group experience provides an outlet for those students.

A Student Insists on Listening to Music While Doing Individual Work or Homework

During parent conferences, parents often complain that their child insists on playing music while doing homework. Please note, this is different from watching television while "working," which is meant as a distraction. In light of multiple intelligences theory, students who insist on working with music playing in the background may not be trying to be off-task, but rather, they may have a high musical intelligence. Low music in the background may actually help activate cognitive functions in these students (see Box 7.2 for an adult example of this phenomenon). Students with a high intelligence in this area who are not permitted to listen to low music, but are forced to simply sit quietly and work quietly, may "turn-off" cognitively or become truly off-task.

How does one deal with this type of student?

Music would cause a disturbance during classroom work time for the non–high musical intelligence students. However, playing music in the classroom during breaks or passing periods, or when students enter the classroom, may help cognitively energize these students. Sharing this information with the parents, suggesting that they allow their child to listen to low music as they work—levels that would not obviously disrupt others or significantly distract the student—may actually help these students stay on task and improve the quality of their assignments. In cooperative work group experiences, playing classical music in the background activates these students, and usually will not adversely affect the non-musical students as they are involved in the group process.

There are many other "noncurricular," practical applications for the direct incorporation of multiple intelligence theory into the classroom. Although these are not applicable to the cooperative work group experience, they are a central part of the overall classroom environment. A key area of attention may be during standardized testing. Unfortunately, standardized testing is almost completely linguistic-based, and to a lesser point, logical-mathematical based. Even though there is no difference in cognitive ability, students who have a high level in these intelligence areas will typically do better on standardized tests than those who are weak in these two areas.

But what about those with high multiple intelligence levels in the other areas? Obviously, the standardized test itself cannot be altered for these students. However, the teacher can adapt the testing *environment* to help activate them cognitively, before and during the testing situation, thereby ultimately contributing to a higher test score.

The following are easy, practical suggestions that can be incorporated into the testing classroom in order to reach these particular students. Although these ideas are not a guarantee of increased success on these exams, still, for some students, they may help better align the testing environment to an arena where they can better reach their cognitive potential.

For students with a high spatial intelligence, place pictures or designs on the walls directly in front of them. These should be items not normally present in the classroom, so that they will immediately stimulate some visual interest. The teacher should also provide these students with scratch paper on which to doodle. For legal and security reasons, the scratch papers are to be collected and returned with the testing materials, similar to the procedures conducted during the math portions of the test.

For students with a high bodily-kinesthetic intelligence, the teacher can allow them to have a quiet, squeeze-type object in their hand while they are testing. The teacher should also ensure that these students move around the class during any free time between test sections.

For students with a high musical intelligence, the teacher can play quiet music in the classroom, both when the students enter, and also during any test breaks.

For students with a high interpersonal intelligence, the teacher should allow them to sit near their friends during the test. This is, of course, a highly controversial position.

However, consider that although conversing during the test is forbidden, the proximity to others with whom they have an interpersonal relationship may activate these students cognitively. Above all, do not place a high "interpersonal" student in isolation during the test, for it could prove to be counter-productive. Another strategy would be to allow these students time to talk to their friends during break times or in-between test sections.

For students with a high intrapersonal intelligence, the teacher should allow them to sit by themselves in a more "private" section of the room, or at a minimum, have them sit at the end of a row where they have one less person near them. This allows these students to reflect better on a personal basis, without experiencing an obtrusiveness from others in close proximity.

For students with a high naturalist intelligence, the teacher should place their desks near a window or positioned in some fashion where they can look out and see trees, grass, and other vegetation. If this arrangement is not feasible, then place them next to a classroom animal or aquarium, or near a plant. If this is still not an option, post pictures or posters of nature in their view so that they can easily look at them, and be energized by the natural setting, during the test.

All of these suggestions require a minimum of environmental manipulation by the teacher. It is inevitably up to the teacher to determine how best to meet the combined needs of the individual students, the required curriculum, and the specific teaching situation. Integration of the multiple intelligences into the classroom environment is highly worthwhile, for they may stimulate the thinking processes of the individual students in both whole class and cooperative work group experiences.

One of the three basic areas of the cooperative work group concept is to determine ways for the students to best reach their cognitive potential—a quality that is important in today's highly competitive business world. By being aware, and actively manipulating, the use of multiple intelligence theory in the classroom, teachers can assist students in reaching this goal. It is one tool, among many, that teachers can keep in their teaching repertoire to use in enhancing student learning and achievement, while simultaneously addressing individual difficulties and problems.

PUTTING THEORY INTO PRACTICE: ADDRESSING THE STUDENTS' MULTIPLE INTELLIGENCES

In addition to the analyzation of his students' multiple intelligence levels, Mr. Washington also manipulated his classroom environment to help intellectually stimulate all of his students. He tried to arrange and include in his classroom whatever was needed to actively promote the cognitive abilities of every individual.

During his cooperative work group experience on assisting the homeless, Mr. Washington arranged his room to address each of the following intelligences:

- For the high *linguistic* intelligence students, he posted different direct quotes and popular news bites, such as: *"1,000,000 CHILDREN IN AMERICA GO TO BED HUNGRY EVERY NIGHT."*

- For the high *logical-mathematical* intelligence students, he posted a "financial reality" chart. The chart showed a realistic monthly income for a homeless person who worked full-time (determined by forty hours multiplied by minimum wage multiplied by four weeks). From the total was subtracted one month's rent for a one-bedroom apartment, the cost of minimal monthly food requirements for a family of four, minimum living expenses (e.g., utilities), and finally, the one month required security deposit for a new apartment. The result was a negative number, which explained why some homeless remained homeless, though employed.

- For the high *spatial* intelligence students, he posted a number of pictures of homeless families, keying in on families with children.

- For the high *bodily-kinesthetic* intelligence students, he randomly distributed research and work materials around the room, forcing the students to physically move to obtain the materials to work on their project.

- For the high *musical* intelligence students, he had protest-music, or music supporting a cause or an idea such as the civil rights movement, playing every day when the students entered the classroom, such as selections recorded by Bob Dylan and Tracy Chapman.

- For the high *naturalist* intelligence students, he paired pictures of farmland with those of inner-city homeless people. He also had a small dirt box (two feet by two feet) in which he was growing vegetables—to be eaten by a homeless person.

- Mr. Washington dealt with the *intrapersonal* and *interpersonal* intelligences through the actual work of the cooperative work groups and their individual projects and tasks.

By manipulating his classroom environment, Mr. Washington was able to ensure that every one of the multiple intelligences were promoted in some fashion within the physical confines of the room, thereby encouraging the cognitive processes of each individual student.

NOTES

1. For example, an ERIC search using just the term "Brain Research" provided well over 300 separate references; the term *multiple intelligences* brought in more than 300 additional references.

2. Please note that there are many different theories of how a child's brain functions—many of which are contradictory to each other. Gardner's theory, while it has its numerous supporters, also has its critics. For an example of a contrary opinion, please refer to Klein, 1997.

3. For an easy-to-read, detailed explanation of each of the intelligences, including how they were derived, and how they can individually be integrated into a classroom's curriculum, please refer to *Multiple Intelligences in the Classroom*, Armstrong, 2000.

4. A "twelve-inch voice" is a term used when students speak at a low enough level where they are audible only to someone who is sitting no more than twelve inches away. It is an excellent tool to use when there are many cooperative groups working within a single classroom.

Teacher Use of the Multiple Intelligences

The classroom teacher is ultimately the best one to determine a student's multiple intelligence levels. This information can lead to improved student performance and improved classroom management in both whole class and cooperative work group settings. Determining a student's multiple intelligence level is a skill that evolves as the teacher gets to know his or her students, their individual work habits, personalities, and learning preferences. This determination is accomplished in two ways, each relevant at a different time of the year:

- Give the students a multiple intelligences test at the beginning of the year.

- Do an analysis of the students' multiple intelligences a few months into the year, when familiar with and appreciative of all the students at a higher level.

A multiple intelligence test is a very simple one-page test that can be administered in ten to fifteen minutes. It can be scored immediately and interpreted by either the students or the teacher, or both. The assessment asks the students to rate how well they enjoy certain activities. Students with a high multiple intelligence in particular areas tend to enjoy certain activities that exemplify that intelligence. See, for example, Figure 8.1.

In a typical multiple intelligence test, the students choose their preferences from a list of age-appropriate activities. The teacher then notes how many of these activities were selected in each of the individual intelligences. The more activities selected, the higher that particular intelligence; the fewer activities selected, the lower that intelligence. Most often, a student will show both high and low scores in one or two areas. Two popular examples of student multiple intelligence tests have been included in Resource B. These tests may be reproduced for classroom use.

The second means of assessing the students' multiple intelligence levels is through conducting a multiple intelligences inventory. This is a checklist the teacher completes privately and is based on personal knowledge of the student. Obviously, this type of assessment cannot be conducted until the teacher is familiar with, and appreciative of, the particular students being assessed. However, a growing trend in schools that actively incorporate multiple intelligence theory into their curricula, is for teachers to include the information in the students' cumulative record (often in the "teacher comments" section) for use by the following year's teacher. This alleviates the "wait time" necessary for teachers to assess their new students.

When in possession of a multiple intelligence inventory, the teacher can reflect on a particular student, marking off displayed tendencies, as well as other manifestations

Figure 8.1   Determining the Students' Multiple Intelligences

If the student has a high . . .	*He or she would most likely enjoy . . .*
Linguistic intelligence	Word games
Logical-mathematical intelligence	Number games
Spatial intelligence	Art activities
Bodily-kinesthetic intelligence	Drama activities, dancing, or sports
Musical intelligence	Playing an instrument
Interpersonal intelligence	Peer tutoring
Intrapersonal intelligence	Keeping a journal
Naturalist intelligence	Going on hikes

of that intelligence. This type of assessment can be easily developed by any teacher who has a good working knowledge of the multiple intelligences, taking into account the specific age-level and interests of the students.

Some multiple intelligence inventories have already been created for teacher use. An excellent one has been written and published by Armstrong in his book *Multiple Intelligences in the Classroom* (2000, pp. 24–27). This inventory is reproduced with permission and can be found in Resource B.

Once the basic intelligence levels of the students are determined, the results should be recorded in the teacher roll book to be readily accessible. It is suggested to color-code each intelligence (e.g., linguistic, red; logical-mathematical, green; etc.), with strengths noted by a colored dot in one column and weaknesses in another column. Be aware that some students may have two or three "dots" noted as a strength and/or a weakness. Conversely, some students may not have any marks, not being extremely strong or weak in any one area. This also provides you with an easy-to-access reference when formulating cooperative work groups.

Note that every student has all of the multiple intelligences to some level and degree. Some are higher or lower than others. Some students may not show a dominating intelligence in any area. However, noting an above-average strength or weakness is important for two reasons:

• It allows a teacher to diagnose potential academic problems with certain students, such as that related in the opening anecdote for Part II.

• It allows a teacher to use a student's strength in specific activities, such as when the student is assigned to a particular cooperative work group.

To accomplish these two tasks effectively, it is important that strict standards of interpretation be determined prior to the assessment. For example, one of the student multiple intelligence tests included in Resource B operates on a scale of 0–5 ("0" being the lowest expression of that particular intelligence, "5" the highest expression of that particular intelligence). The scores using this assessment would be interpreted as shown in Figure 8.2.

Figure 8.2   Profiling Student Strengths and Weaknesses

Student Multiple Intelligence Test Score	Strength or Weakness	Teacher Note in the Roll Book
5	Very strong	Score is noted
4	Strong	Score is noted if student has no "5's" in any other area
3	Average	Score is not noted
2	Average	Score is not noted
1	Weak	Score is noted if student has no "0's" in any other area
0	Very weak	Score is noted

By noting these strengths and weaknesses and keeping the information readily accessible when necessary, it can be referred to immediately. As a result, cooperative work groups are quickly enhanced; student problems may be rapidly diagnosed. It is to the potential of using the multiple intelligences to help solve individual student learning problems that this text now turns.

One useful aspect of this theory is that knowledge of the students' multiple intelligence levels may help alleviate many student learning problems. For example, if the teacher notices that a student is having difficulty in an academic area, the curricular material can be adapted or placed in a context that better matches the student's highest multiple intelligence. In this fashion, the teacher is presenting the information in a way or a context in which the student's brain is better stimulated. This will not resolve all, or maybe even most, academic difficulties the teacher encounters. However, it still is one tool that can help alleviate and address some of the problems.

For example, imagine a student working in a cooperative work group on a language arts project involving the life and works of Mark Twain. The student is experiencing difficulty understanding the connection between the various themes that run through Twain's literature. This situation is subsequently causing a problem for the student in understanding, analyzing, and ultimately completing the work assigned within the group. In order to assist this student, the teacher would first look in the roll book to ascertain the student's highest multiple intelligence level. Depending on that level, the teacher might incorporate one of the teaching tactics in Figure 8.3.

Notice in Figure 8.3 that in some areas the curricular material can easily be presented in that particular mode (linguistic, logical-mathematical, interpersonal, intrapersonal), while in others, the teacher is manipulating the student's environment in some fashion (spatial, bodily-kinesthetic, musical, naturalist). However, in all of these scenarios, the ultimate teacher goal is both to activate the student's thinking power and for the student to understand better the previously unclear material through the direct integration of the students' highest multiple intelligence levels.

On an expanded basis, teachers can incorporate the multiple intelligences into their curricula in order to effectively activate the students' thinking processes, and ultimately to help them learn curricular material. By actively adapting the educational

Figure 8.3 Strategies for Using the Multiple Intelligences to Solve Student Academic Difficulties

If the student has a high . . .	The teacher would use this strategy for helping the student understand the theme of the literature piece:
Linguistic intelligence	Verbally explain the various themes to the student in a variety of ways, using different examples from Twain's works and similar plots and literary devices found in his other stories.
Logical-mathematical intelligence	Draw a type of flow chart on the board connecting the various themes that Twain used and how they are logically manifested within the plots of his different stories.
Spatial intelligence	Locate a couple of pictures showing scenes that could be from one of Twain's books. Using the pictures as a visual guide to stimulate discussion, explaining how the theme is developed through the story.
Bodily-kinesthetic intelligence	Take a walk with the student anywhere on campus (such as on an errand to the office), or participate in a physical activity such as shooting some baskets. During this physical movement opportunity, discuss the themes with the student.
Musical intelligence	Put on some non-distracting music in the background and discuss the thematic material with the student. For older students, ask them to write a verse and chorus for a song describing the theme.
Interpersonal intelligence	Pair a student with a friend who understands the thematic material, and have them peer-tutor. If time permits within the cooperative work group activity, have the entire group discuss the material that is confusing.
Intrapersonal intelligence	Provide the student with some similar excerpts with the same themes, and/or some personal questions for reflection. Ask the student to go home and reflect on the questions.
Naturalist intelligence	Go outside with the student, sit under a tree or in some other natural setting, and discuss the theme. Have the student create a picture in his or her mind of Twain sitting by the Mississippi River, developing his themes and plots.

Figure 8.4   Mr. Washington's Roll Book Marked With the Multiple Intelligences

Name	High Multiple Intelligence					Low Multiple Intelligence				
Alberto	▦					░	▥			
Andrew	▨									
Ashlee	░	▥				▦				
Cari	▤									
Carla	░	▥				▨				
Daniel	▩					▨				
Elizabeth	░					▤				
Freddy	▨	▨				▧				
Gaby	▧	▥				░				
Gordon	▨									

Key:

░	Linguistic Intelligence
▨	Logical-Mathematical Intelligence
▧	Spatial Intelligence
▤	Bodily-Kinesthetic Intelligence
▨	Musical Intelligence
▥	Interpersonal Intelligence
▦	Intrapersonal Intelligence
▩	Naturalist Intelligence

material to the personal learning styles of the students, or by ensuring that every one of the intelligences is accounted for within the curricular setting, the students have an enhanced opportunity to reach their learning potential within the classroom. This type of enriched curricular environment is especially applicable to the cooperative work group experience.

PUTTING THEORY INTO PRACTICE: DETERMINING THE STUDENTS' MULTIPLE INTELLIGENCES

Mr. Washington had given all of his students a simple multiple intelligences test. On the first page of his roll book, he color-coded each of the intelligences, and listed the highest areas of each of the students, based on his previous analysis. Adjacent to this list, he used the same color-coding to note the areas where the individual students were extremely weak. For example, the linguistic intelligence might be marked in red ink, logical-mathematical intelligence might be in blue, green could be used for the spatial intelligence, and so on. Figure 8.4 is an example of part of Mr. Washington's roll book as marked with the students' highest and lowest multiple intelligences levels.

With this information at hand, Mr. Washington was able to easily and immediately consider the students' various multiple intelligence strengths and weaknesses both when he established the groups and throughout various phases appropriate to classroom management issues.

Integrating the Multiple Intelligences Into Cooperative Work Group Experiences

LOOKING AT THE CLASSROOM HOLISTICALLY

The cooperative work group concept must be considered in a holistic fashion within the overall classroom curriculum. It is a teaching methodology that assists the students with solving problems and completing curricular projects. However, it does not "operate in a vacuum." It is not an end-all in and of itself. "Teaching"—often frontal—occurs prior to, and subsequent to, the group experience.

In the same light, the multiple intelligences must be considered when helping the students reach their thinking potential; during both the actual cooperative work group process, and during the parts of the curricula delivered before and after. Most of the teaching suggestions that follow can be applied both to work completed within the cooperative work group experience and to that completed during other components of the overall curriculum.

Since every student has different and varying high and low multiple intelligences, thinks in a distinct way, and is cognitively activated in a particular fashion, the teacher needs to ensure that all of the multiple intelligences are represented at some point, in some fashion, in every curricular unit.

At the same time, it is rather unreasonable to try to place each of the multiple intelligences into every lesson, especially when dealing with periods of less than an hour in length (the teacher would have virtually no time to teach the required curriculum). It is also somewhat impractical to fully integrate the intelligences into every subject area (there are few really good songs about quadratic equations). Still, if the teacher views the entire curriculum in "units," the multiple intelligences can easily be integrated somewhere within the overall learning experience.

The same general concept applies when integrating the multiple intelligences into cooperative work group experiences. Most of the intelligences can be incorporated into the actual work of the individual groups. However, those that are not can still be covered within the various curricular learning experiences taking place prior and subsequent to the actual cooperative work group activity. This planning process is identical to that accomplished by the classroom teacher at other times in the year.

There are three basic strategies teachers can use to fully integrate the multiple intelligences into both the classroom curricula and the cooperative work group experiences:

- Using the multiple intelligences in the presentation of curricular material

- Using the multiple intelligences in the creative work of the students

- Using the multiple intelligences in the construction of the classroom environment

USING THE MULTIPLE INTELLIGENCES IN THE PRESENTATION OF CURRICULAR MATERIAL

Various components of each of the individual multiple intelligences can be integrated into every curricular unit with a little teacher creativity. In an extensive cooperative work group experience, this planning process will probably have been completed based on the various tasks and teaching modalities that are normally included within this type of teaching methodology. This is especially the case when the cooperative work groups are dealing with material that is supplemental to the core curriculum (see the chapters in Part I for a discussion of the various types of goals of a cooperative work group experience). Usually, good planning and teaching will naturally cover most of the multiple intelligences.

There are three basic steps for the teacher to undertake when planning a unit that will ensure that all of the multiple intelligences are covered somewhere within the learning experience:

- First, plan normally the cooperative work group experience—goals, activities, assessment, and so on.

- Second, use a multiple intelligences chart to determine if, and where, all of the intelligences have been integrated within the overall unit.

- Third, plan for an expression/application of any of the multiple intelligences that have been omitted, per the information provided by the chart.

A multiple intelligence chart is a very simple table that can be created by the teacher. Its purpose is to check to see if all of the intelligences have been covered within the normal curricular planning. With a multiple intelligence chart, the teacher has only to note an example of where the students will use, or be exposed to, that particular intelligence within the overall learning experience. Not every instance of each intelligence needs to be charted. Quite the contrary. Chances are that in an extensive unit, if an intelligence is being actively used, it will be incorporated in a variety of ways. The goal of the chart is only to ensure that some form of every intelligence is used during the overall unit. This can occur either before, during, or after the actual cooperative work group experience.

Figure 9.1 is an example of a multiple intelligence chart that was created during the planning for a cooperative work group experience on pioneer life in the late 1800s.

Figure 9.1   Multiple Intelligence Chart for Pioneer Life in the 1800s Unit

Multiple Intelligence	Places where it is covered within the unit
Linguistic intelligence	Reading the book *Sarah, Plain and Tall* (Maclachlan, 1985); reading material found on the Internet
Logical-mathematical intelligence	Planning out the culminating County Fair activity—exploring various items, manipulating data and materials
Spatial intelligence	Looking at pictures of pioneer life used as data sources throughout the cooperative work group experience
Bodily-kinesthetic intelligence	Learning and performing a country dance during the County Fair activity
Musical intelligence	Learning a pioneer song that was discovered during Internet research and performing it during the County Fair activity
Interpersonal intelligence	The actual cooperative work group experience
Intrapersonal intelligence	Individual work on booths for the County Fair activity; during individual research as a member of a cooperative work group
Naturalist intelligence	Using information discovered during the cooperative work group research pertaining to the natural resources used by the pioneers

The chart includes learning activities before, during, and after the actual cooperative work group experience. For example, the primary linguistic activity was conducted before the cooperative work group sessions began, and was the catalyst for the final project—a "county fair." The actual group sessions entailed the active use of the linguistic, logical-mathematical, spatial, musical, interpersonal, intrapersonal, and naturalist intelligences. Logical-mathematical, bodily-kinesthetic, and intrapersonal intelligences were used in class sessions after the group time.

There were invariably many other manifestations of the multiple intelligences throughout the unit that were not listed in this chart. The important aspect is that the teacher makes sure that at least one experience is included for each of the intelligences somewhere during the unit.

Whereas most of the individual intelligences were naturally part of the extended history unit above, a chart is especially useful for subject areas that do not readily address the various multiple intelligences—for example, math and science. With these curricular areas, a multiple intelligence chart helps the teacher focus on all of the areas. Figure 9.2 contains one such chart created for a unit on fractions.

It follows that after the chart is created, if one of the areas is blank, the teacher needs to locate or create a learning experience for that particular intelligence. For example, a

Figure 9.2 Multiple Intelligence Chart for Fractions Unit

Multiple Intelligence	*Places where it is covered within the unit*
Linguistic intelligence	Reading the book *Math Curse* (Scieszka, 1995); reading material found throughout the unit
Logical-mathematical Intelligence	The math from the fractions unit itself
Spatial intelligence	Charts and pictures showing fractions
Bodily-kinesthetic intelligence	Physically dividing the students into various groupings as part of a "fractions game" demonstrating equivalent fractions
Musical intelligence	Having a discussion on time signatures in music and how they are similar to fractions (e.g., number of units in a measure over the unit itself)
Interpersonal intelligence	The actual cooperative work group experience
Intrapersonal intelligence	Individual work on material within the unit; during individual research as a member of a cooperative work group
Naturalist intelligence	A final project where the students "plan the use of a new park." They are given acreage and fractions of how they are to use it (e.g., 1/6 blacktop basketball courts), and then must design it.

teacher is creating a unit on the life and times of Shakespeare. After planning out the unit, a multiple intelligences chart is made and completed. Unexpectedly, there is nothing included in the musical intelligence category. The teacher would then search for some aspect or activity that would cover this particular area. This may include listening to examples of music created during this period of history or from a musical Broadway show based on the work of Shakespeare, or by having the students write a song to go with one of Shakespeare's plays or sonnets.

Either way, by incorporating a multiple intelligences chart the teacher can ensure that all of the areas are covered, and if one is missing, address its incorporation into the unit.

USING THE MULTIPLE INTELLIGENCES IN THE CREATIVE WORK OF STUDENTS

The multiple intelligences can also be incorporated into the creative work of the students. This is especially true when students have an extensive, open-ended final

Figure 9.3   Individual Projects for a Unit on Pioneer Life in the 1800s

If the student has a high . . .	The student can create the following project using material discovered during the cooperative work group sessions:
Linguistic intelligence	Write a creative story about a pioneer family, specifically incorporating characteristics of everyday life at this time.
Logical-mathematical intelligence	Create a step-by-step manual on how to establish a settlement, one that could be used by prospective pioneers moving west.
Spatial intelligence	Create a brochure on pioneer life that demonstrates various characteristics of pioneer life for prospective pioneers moving west.
Bodily-kinesthetic intelligence	Create and perform a dance, or write and perform a scene, that incorporates and explains various characteristics of pioneer life.
Musical intelligence	Write lyrics to, and perform, an original or previously recorded song that explains various characteristics of pioneer life.
Interpersonal intelligence	Work together with another person and plan a detailed model of a new pioneer community.
Intrapersonal intelligence	Write a personal diary based either on a character from the *Sarah, Plain and Tall* book, or create a new fictional pioneer character.
Naturalist Intelligence	Investigate and list the various natural resources in a specific pioneer area and tell how they would each be used by the pioneers in the various facets of their lives.

project to plan and complete, similar to the type of culminating activity planned by Mr. Washington and his students in the earlier anecdote.

There are two basic reasons to encourage, or insist, that students use the various intelligences during a creative project:

• It allows those students with a high multiple intelligence in nontraditionally tested areas (those other than linguistic and logical-mathematical) to have an opportunity to demonstrate what they have learned in an assessment mode that is best suited to their thinking processes.

• It provides active practice for those who have a weakness in one or more of the multiple intelligences. Whereas everyone is basically high or low in particular areas, one's abilities can be strengthened through exposure in particular intelligences.

There are many ways that students can demonstrate their knowledge—assessment—through the incorporation of the multiple intelligences. For instance, Figure 9.3 provides some examples of individual projects that students could complete during

Figure 9.4 Individual Projects for a Unit on Fractions

If the student has a high . . .	The student can create the following project using material discovered during the cooperative work group sessions:
Linguistic intelligence	Write a creative story about the daily use of fractions, for example, "A Day in Fraction Land."
Logical-mathematical intelligence	Develop various charts demonstrating knowledge of the different formulas used throughout the fractions unit.
Spatial intelligence	Using fractional directions, draw the floor plan for a house (e.g., the living room is 1/4 of the house).
Bodily-kinesthetic intelligence	Create and perform a scene or activity where the students continually divide themselves into fractional units.
Musical intelligence	Write a few measures and explain the rhythm of music that is in various time signatures: 4/4, 3/4, 2/4, 6/8, 5/8
Interpersonal intelligence	Work together with another person to create a housing development based on fractions, similar to the idea in the Spatial Intelligence section above
Intrapersonal intelligence	Have the student go through the day and mark all activities, then figure out the fractional equivalents of how the day was spent (e.g., 1/4 of the day was spent in school).
Naturalist Intelligence	Using fractions, investigate facets of the rain forest: what amount is used by various species or natives, how much is being destroyed every day.

the previously mentioned cooperative work group experience on pioneer life in the 1800s. In this type of assessment, the students are allowed to use their highest multiple intelligence in the development of something creative that exemplifies their understanding of pioneer life during this time period.

This type of assessment—through use of the multiple intelligences—is also useful in determining whether or not student have overall knowledge of concepts, versus relying on the standard testing of specific facts and skills (such is often found in math or science classes). Figure 9.4 provides an example of the various types of multiple intelligence-based assessments that could be used with the fractions unit noted above.

What differentiates these activities from typical curricular assessment is twofold:

- All of these projects were the choice of the student, versus a directive of the teacher.

- The individual project choices were based on the cognitive strengths of the student, versus typical linguistic-based or logical-mathematical–based assessments.

The key to the success of these types of assessment is ensuring that the students are previously aware of the concept of the multiple intelligences and, having taken a prior test, already know their basic strengths and weaknesses. They are then able to create their own, personal final project in their area of expertise, demonstrating their basic knowledge of the overall curricular concepts. This type of assessment does not necessarily replace traditional testing, but can be used as a supplement for the teacher. This could prove to be especially useful for students who do not perform well using standardized types of tests, even though they understand the basic concepts.

On the other side, the teacher can use a curricular final project to provide a variety of new multiple intelligences experiences for the students. This is particularly helpful when that teacher wants to provide the students with an opportunity to strengthen their weaker areas of intelligences. Providing practice and experience of this sort is especially important in the elementary and middle school years when students are crystallizing their work and study habits and their cognitive abilities.

For example, continuing with the pioneer unit discussed above, the teacher can give the students the following prompt for an individualized final project:

> You are going to create a three-dimensional display of some aspect of pioneer life in the late 1800s, which will become part of our classroom country fair. The display should include a poster of information (various facts and pictures), along with artifacts that were used, or could have been used, during that time period. You can also personally demonstrate some feature of pioneer life as part of your display.
>
> You are required to use at least five of the following six multiple intelligences in your project:
>
> - Linguistic
> - Logical-mathematical
> - Spatial
> - Bodily-kinesthetic
> - Musical
> - Naturalist
>
> Refer to your classroom notes on the types of projects and information that each of these multiple intelligence areas encompasses.

This type of final project/assessment forces the students to use multiple intelligence areas in which they may not be either strong or ordinarily comfortable. Simultaneously, by *not* requiring the use of *all* of the areas, the students are not unnecessarily burdened with an intelligence with which they are either truly uncomfortable (such as areas where they scored a "0" on their multiple intelligence test), or an area that does not easily integrate into the project that they wish to create.

Please also note that the intrapersonal and interpersonal areas are not included in the prompt. These two intelligences are more apt to be used within the teaching environment (individual work or the cooperative work group experience) and are therefore less apt to be controlled or manipulated by the student.

In either case, using multiple intelligences in the creative work of the students provides a more valid assessment of their knowledge and ability, while at the same time strengthening their personal cognitive abilities. These types of activities are appropriate in cooperative work group experiences and for many of the ordinary assessments that occur within the everyday classroom curricula.

USING THE MULTIPLE INTELLIGENCES IN THE CONSTRUCTION OF THE CLASSROOM ENVIRONMENT

Oftentimes the subject matter or time frame of the curricular unit does not lend itself to the integration of each of the intelligences. A unit on chemistry or verb conjugations, or a one- to two-period lesson, may not provide the opportunity to ensure that all of the intelligences are covered within the particular teaching situation. In those instances, the only way to adequately integrate the multiple intelligences into the curriculum for that specific unit is through the manipulation of the classroom environment.

The classroom environment includes not only the physical layout of the room (materials on walls and arrangement of desks), but also the basic learning environment. This concept encompasses the entire spectrum of teaching methodologies from frontal teaching to cooperative learning.

As previously mentioned, some subjects do not lend themselves to all of the intelligences, or sometimes a project is not extensive enough to incorporate all of the intelligences. It is unreasonable to expect the classroom teacher to spend time to artificially create ways to cover each of the multiple intelligences. However, in those teaching situations, it is important to somehow touch on all of the areas, for no other reason than to help activate the students' individual cognitive processes.

Although this method of manipulating the classroom environment may not be as beneficial as directly presenting the curricular material through each of the intelligences, still, it will help in stimulating to some degree the students' thinking processes.

The following are some examples of how each of the multiple intelligences can be provided for the students through adapting the overall environment within the classroom. Some possibilities directly relate to one's teaching methods, some to the physical layout of the room itself. In particular, each of them is geared toward adapting the overall classroom environment during a cooperative work group activity, in order to specifically address each of the multiple intelligences:

The *linguistic intelligence* is quite easy to use, since it is inevitably the core of the vast majority of curricular units. Written material and group discussions cover this intelligence. In addition, the debriefing section at the end of each of the work sessions (refer to Chapter 6) can include a verbal overview of the material covered on that particular day.

The *logical-mathematical intelligence* can also be addressed within the lesson. Graphic organizers can be given to each student at the beginning of the cooperative work group session. The design should display what the various groups are doing within the total project, and how each task relates to the others. During the debriefing session, the teacher can create a flow chart on the board showing the same process, graphically representing where the students are within the overall project.

The *spatial intelligence* is incorporated by manipulating the physical classroom environment. The teacher can display pictures and posters around the room, each of which relates to the topic. These works will stimulate the thinking processes of students with high intelligence in this area. Another way is to ensure that each group is provided with pictorial material. This can easily be accomplished through the use of the vertical file system (see Chapter 4).

The *bodily-kinesthetic intelligence* is addressed through having the students periodically alter the physical arrangement of the seats and/or themselves. Rather than having students shift chairs to face a particular direction, either have them stand and move into groups, move back to a whole-class situation for a debriefing session, or require them to walk to different parts of the room for materials and supplies. For extended work sessions (those longer than an hour), it is imperative that there be a break in the middle so those who need this movement can stand up and move around. This can be accomplished in an elementary school by having a cooperative work session occur before and after recess and lunch. In secondary schools, where block scheduling occurs, this can be incorporated by allowing the students to leave the room during passing periods. The key is to find or create time where the students who require this type of stimulation can be physically moving during their extended work period.

The *musical intelligence* is a more difficult one to incorporate into the classroom environment, unless the topic is being dealt with musically, either directly within the lesson or within the group tasks. When this is not the case, the easiest way to address this intelligence is to have some music playing both when the students enter the room and during the same break periods discussed above under "Bodily-Kinesthetic Intelligence."

The *interpersonal intelligence* is by definition incorporated into the classroom environment through the use of the entire cooperative work group concept.

The *intrapersonal intelligence* can be addressed by ensuring that there is a portion of each project when students are working alone. This can be accomplished via a personal investigation of data, or as an additional assessment created by the individual students. It can also be dealt with through the use of personal student journals and "warm-up prompts" at the beginning of the class period.

The *naturalist intelligence* is problematic to incorporate when it is not directly an integral component of that particular curriculum. Manipulation of the physical environment is the easiest way to address this intelligence and can be accomplished in a number of ways. A cooperative work group with a number of naturalist-strong students can be allowed to do some of their group work outside on a grassy area. This group may be cognitively energized by being out in a nature-based environment. Another way is to have plants and/or animals as part of the classroom environment, with work areas nearby for those students who wish to take advantage of this natural retreat. Finally, if there are pictures with a naturalist theme that would correlate with the subject matter, they can be posted within the classroom to stimulate these students' thinking processes.

An additional way for the teacher to incorporate the multiple intelligences specifically into the cooperative work group classroom environment is through the active manipulation of the group formation procedures, as is described in Part I. This is a relatively simple two-part process:

• Determine which specific multiple intelligence characteristics are important to each of the individual groups.

• Refer to the roll book for which students have a high multiple intelligence in that particular area, and assign them to that particular group (refer to Figure 8.4 in Chapter 8 for an example).

By using the multiple intelligences in all portions of the educational program— the presentation of curricular materials, the creative work of the students, and the construction of the classroom environment—the teacher can ensure that students' needs are being addressed in order to reach their cognitive potential, and therefore be productive members of the cooperative work groups. Ultimately, as the students mature and eventually become contributing members of the adult workforce, they

Figure 9.5   Matching Students' Multiple Intelligence Levels to the Cooperative Work Group

Cooperative Work Groups Established	Appropriate Multiple Intelligence Levels	Students Most Appropriate for This Group[1]	Students to Avoid Placing in This Group
Drama	Bodily-kinesthetic	Cari	Elizabeth
Music	Musical Bodily-kinesthetic	Cari, Freddy, Gordon	Daniel, Elizabeth
Literature	Linguistic	Ashlee, Carla, Elizabeth	Alberto
Brochure, Investigation	Logical-mathematics. Naturalist	Andrew, Daniel, Freddy	Carla, Gaby
Brochure, Publication	Spatial	Gaby	Freddy

NOTE: 1. Only the students listed in Figure 8.4 are included in this chart, not all of the students in Mr. Washington's class.

will develop self-realization and build upon their multiple intelligence strengths to be effective as they work on extended projects in the business world.

PUTTING THEORY INTO PRACTICE: USING THE MULTIPLE INTELLIGENCES IN GROUP FORMATION

To demonstrate this procedure, refer back to Chapter 2, Figure 2.4, Mr. Washington's First Grouping Worksheet, where he used the multiple intelligences as one of his grouping variables.

With this information in his roll book (see Figure 8.4 in Chapter 8), Mr. Washington was able to formulate more efficient cooperative work groups, student units that included members required for the particular tasks of that group. He was able to immediately determine which student multiple intelligences would be an asset for a particular group, and which low intelligences would potentially become a hindrance to the group goals.

Since his multiple intelligence goals for the cooperative work group experience were curricular in nature, versus being designed to give experience and support for the students' weaker intelligences, Mr. Washington wanted to create well-functioning groups. Based on this readily available data, he was able to make the following determinations based on the students listed in Figure 9.5.

A caution, even though this list directed Mr. Washington toward specific group formations, he had earlier determined that the multiple intelligence levels were but one aspect of group formation. Other student variables needed to be taken into account as he took a holistic view of how to create the cooperative work groups. For example, Daniel had a high naturalist intelligence, which had been determined to be an asset for the Brochure Group (Investigation). However, he did not get along at all well with Melvin and Olivia, both of whom were important for that group. Washington also considered that since Olivia had a high naturalist intelligence, it was not necessary for Daniel to be placed within that group. Therefore, based on those two variables, Daniel was assigned to a different group.

The multiple intelligences were simply one important variable, among many, that Mr. Washington incorporated into the planning and implementation of his successful cooperative group work experience.

A FINAL NOTE

Today's brain research—in this instance, the theory of the multiple intelligences—can best help teachers assist their students in achieving their cognitive potential. By discovering efficient ways to cognitively energize the students, and providing them with the opportunity to learn and function in that fashion, the teacher enables the students to operate at peak cognitive proficiency, becoming the most productive students that they can individually be.

There are many ways that the teacher can incorporate multiple intelligences theory into the cooperative work group process:

• By determining each student's personal strengths and weaknesses, the information can be used to evaluate learning difficulties and help promote every student's individual learning potential.

• By integrating each of the intelligences into the presentation of curricular material, the students each have greater opportunities to access the information in a way that best suits their personal learning styles.

• By allowing the students to pick and choose among the various intelligences in their presentations of their cooperative work group projects, they can better express themselves and demonstrate their own personal learning accomplishments.

Part III

The Internet as the Ultimate Educational Resource Center

PUTTING THEORY INTO PRACTICE: USING THE INFORMATION SUPER-CURRICULUM

As Mr. Washington began planning his cooperative work group project on helping the homeless, he first investigated the different resources that would be available to his students. He knew from experience that unless sufficient curricular resources were available, the project would most likely end in complete failure. A visit to the school library resource center confirmed his fears that there were virtually no on-site resources accessible concerning this topic. Therefore, even before he began the basic work on his unit, he decided to turn to the Internet in order to ascertain whether or not materials and resources existed online for his students to use.

Mr. Washington had a number of highly successful previous experiences locating curricular resources on the Internet. For example, earlier in the year, he had one of his classes conduct a project on the "Gilded Age" of American History (the turn of the twentieth century). The students researched the problems of society and discussed potential new laws that would be appropriate to address those problems.

To start the research for his Gilded Age project, Mr. Washington first went to the Educational Resources page of the general education site, TEACHERS HELPING TEACHERS,[1] and looked under the History/Social Studies section where he discovered a link to

HISTORY/SOCIAL STUDIES WEB SITE FOR K-12 TEACHERS

There, he discovered the following useful Internet sites, all of which supplied curricular material for his students[2]:

Immigration, Ellis Island, page 1. New York, NY, Ellis Island—Immigration: 1900–1920. From University of California, Riverside Keystone-Mast Collection, California Museum of Photography. "Christmas on Ellis Island, ca. 1908."

Triangle Fire. The Triangle Shirtwaist Factory Fire—March 25, 1911. Labor history may be one of the most overlooked topics in American history. For those teachers looking for Web resources, this site offers some needed items. The indexed oral histories were not yet online when I visited, but I located some under the topic of "Sweatshops and Strikes before 1911." You might follow with a visit to the American history sweatshop exhibition at a different location.

Immigration in the Gilded Age and Progressive Era

Gilded Age and Progressive Era. U.S. History Internet Resources . . . an excellent listing.

The Great Homes of America's Gilded Age. Featured homes include: Hearst Castle, Wyntoon, Belcourt Castle, Rosecliff, Breakers, Marble House, The Elms, Fenway Court, Biltmore, Whitehall, Villa Vizcaya, and Ca' d'Zan. All were constructed during a thirty-five–year period from 1890 through 1925.

The Gilded Page. I have often wondered why more English and History departments at the K7–12 don't team teach a unit or two. Here is a page that could easily be used for the literature portion.

Ultimately, Mr. Washington used the Internet as the primary resource in his unit on the Gilded Age. Based on that experience, and others similar to it, he was confident that the Internet would provide sufficient material for his new cooperative work group "Homeless in America" experience.

NOTES

1. To avoid cluttering these pages with long lists of addresses, all Internet site names are given in capital letters, and the URLs are listed in Resource A.

2. Whenever material is reproduced verbatim from an Internet site, the spelling and grammar appear exactly as is displayed on the screen. Unfortunately, all online proofreading is the responsibility of whoever uploads the material onto a Web page.

The Concept, Reality, and Cost of Digital Literacy

DIGITAL LITERACY IN TODAY'S CLASSROOM

Literacy is the "hot" word in education today. The goal of virtually all recent state curricula, and those of the teachers ultimately responsible for the education of the students, is to promote literacy in both reading and math. Another literacy goal has recently been added to curricular guidelines throughout the nation, the goal of literacy in the use of technology, or "digital literacy." Digital literacy, as defined by Paul Glister (1997), is

> the ability to understand information and—more important—to evaluate and integrate information in multiple formats that the computer can deliver. Being able to evaluate and interpret information is critical . . . you can't *understand* information you find on the Internet without evaluating its sources and placing it in context. (p. 6)

The acquisition of digital literacy is critical to the success of the cooperative work group experience. This concept includes the ability of the students to investigate, analyze, evaluate, and directly integrate the vast resources of the Internet into a group project. However, digital literacy does *not* refer to the ability to turn on and correctly operate a computer. Nor does it refer to the ability to use a browser, or to navigate search engines and other online Web sites. Rather, digital literacy among students involves the important features of their critical thinking and work habits:

• Naturally knowing when required curricular information that will help fulfill group goals is available through an online resource

• Having the ability to quickly and efficiently locate that information

• Being able to analyze, evaluate, and ultimately synthesize that information into the goals and requirements of the group project

These three components are critical to the successful work of cooperative work groups in today's information age. Students are expected to know how to use the information provided through online resources. Note that the statement does *not* include "knows how to use online resources." This is an important omission. By the time the students graduate from high school, they know how to use a computer—whether or not they have one at home. Computers have become as commonplace as VCRs in American society. From games to wristwatches, they are a part of everyday life. "Cyberphobia"—the fear of things online—does not exist among today's young generation.

The technological age has also brought about a new, unusual problem—the students often know more about technology than does the teacher. Too often, the classroom teacher is cyberphobic. As a result, an outside person often teaches the class in a school computer lab. Or classroom computers are relegated to an extra "tool" where word processing or CD-ROM games and programs can be played—activities that do not require teacher input. Neither of these scenarios promotes digital literacy in students; neither fully integrates the power of the technological age directly into the teacher-planned, classroom curricula.

The digital literacy of teachers must be addressed. Teachers today must be as knowledgeable and comfortable with online resources as an English teacher is with materials for teaching literature, or a math teacher is with locating mathematical resources. In order to formulate and create successful cooperative work group experiences for their students, teachers need to possess the digital literacy necessary to efficiently and effectively integrate technological resources into their planning.

This skill goes well beyond being adept at using a computer:

Computers often do not live up to their promise because no one shows teachers how to integrate their new technology into their instruction, or, sadly, into their students' learning processes. Thus, when teachers want to go beyond using technology for data input or for motivating youngsters, they face a huge learning hurdle. (Caverly, Peterson, & Mandeville, 1997, p. 56)

Research has shown that the most efficient way to increase the use of higher-order thinking skills through technology (one of the goals of the cooperative work group concept) is *not* through the use of advanced software or hardware. Rather, success in this cognitive area is directly tied to the inservice work of teachers in technological literacy (Latham, 1999). Therefore, the balance of this section is designed to assist teachers in acquiring a measure of digital literacy themselves. The concepts and ideas that are used can then be shared with the students, helping them develop their own digital literacy through cooperative work group experiences.

Today's cyberworld is more extensive than anyone realizes. It seems as if virtually any information that anyone would want to know is available somewhere online. Ultimately, the Internet will prove to be most useful as a resource for teachers and students. The Internet is quietly leading society to a point where schools' curricular materials will no longer be limited due to budgetary constraints. Through use of the Internet, all schools, regardless of socioeconomic status, can have equal access to vast online educational resources.

However, before beginning the discussion on how teachers and students acquire digital literacy, one needs to take into account the current reality of student access to materials on the Internet. This involves determining both the extent and limitations students and teachers currently have to accessing online resources. It is impossible to expect digital literacy to take place without addressing how it can be accomplished within the teacher's and students' educational environment.

The reality is that our society will never attain the educational utopia promoted within political circles—one in which all students have ready and immediate access to online resources at any time during the school day, in any educational setting. The cost is beyond what today's politicians are willing to commit. For example,

> One multi-media–capable, Internet-connected computer for every two or three students yields a price-tag of about $94 billion of initial investment and $28 billion per year in ongoing costs—a financial commitment that would drain schools of all discretionary funding for at least a decade. (Dede, 1997, p. 13)

ESTABLISHING STUDENT ACCESS WITHIN THE SCHOOL

Once the school has Internet access, a key decision is how the school computers will be made accessible to the students. There are a variety of configurations, each with its own strengths and weaknesses, but ultimately the decision will be made by the school's technology budget and other funding sources. *It is the issue of accessibility that will directly shape the structure of the cooperative work group experience.*

Computer access in schools has changed significantly since the late 1990s. Schools used to be limited to twenty to forty computers, which were either placed together in a school computer lab, or parceled out—one or two to each classroom—until they were all distributed. With the infusion of greater amounts of money for school technology budgets, along with a proliferation of teacher technology grant programs, teachers have many more options, and consequently a greater say in how computers are placed within the school. Therefore, it is appropriate to look at the various possibilities and decisions that teachers may have to face—configurations that will directly affect how the cooperative work group concept may be implemented within their classrooms.

There are three basic scenarios for establishing the school's computer program:

- Incorporation of a computer lab
- Use of classroom computer pods
- Placement of one individual computer in a classroom

A Computer Lab

A fully stocked computer lab allows an entire class to work on the computers and on the Internet at one time, via a full lesson, cooperative work groups, or through individual student research. The lab provides for digital literacy to be a fully integrated part of the overall curriculum. The lessons can be directly integrated into the classroom curricula (versus a stand-alone lesson provided solely within the lab, with little or no connection to the classroom curriculum). A computer lab also alleviates teacher cyberphobia if it is managed by a teacher or an aide who knows how to operate the computers and software. A digitally literate instructor teaching the lab lesson would be the best of all possibilities, and would lead to greater integration of the lab work into the classroom curriculum.

The negative aspects of a computer lab are quite significant. The larger the school, the less time available for classes to be in the lab. Spontaneous ideas incorporating the use of the lab are virtually impossible. This type of set-up is not conducive to bringing digital literacy into the curriculum, nor to providing the online information access required in cooperative work group experiences.

A second negative hazard is that by having a lab with special personnel, the cyberphobic teacher is less motivated to become fluent with the digital material, and less likely to plan for its full integration into the classroom curricula.

Classroom Computer Pods

Classroom computer pods are groups of three to five computers placed together in a classroom. Pods are excellent additions because they provide significant computer access for students throughout the year, not just when they can schedule time in the computer lab. Cooperative work groups can be "assigned" to one of the computers, allowing access whenever necessary. Even full classroom lessons can be conducted on these machines when an LCD projector is attached to one of the computers.

The primary purpose of computer pods is to allow for continual individualized student access throughout the year. By having only a few of them in the classroom, they act as a full "center," allowing all students considerable access.

The drawback to classroom computer pods is that without an extraordinary number of school computers (three to five per room), or if the computers were not purchased through a specific grant by that particular teacher, not every faculty member will have equal access. This would severely limit their use in cooperative work group experiences for teachers without the hardware.

Individual Classroom Computers

Another configuration is to place one computer in each classroom. The positive aspect is that there can be access to a computer for all classes throughout the year. The teacher can also link that computer to an LCD projector for a full classroom lesson. Cooperative work groups can "sign up" to use the computer for Internet research during specific time periods.

The negative aspect of this scenario is that computer access is so limited that little significant work can be accomplished. Eventually, what often happens is the computer becomes little more than a "play station" for those who finish their work early, or a place to get homework done in class, rather than at a computer at home.

How the computers are configured within the school is one of the most important decisions that can affect the digital literacy of the students. Ultimately, it will impact how cooperative work groups are able to integrate the Internet resources into their projects. No choice will please everyone. However, if the decisions are tailored to the curricular goals of the school, the decisions made can be fully defended as being educationally sound. The three possible scenarios listed above are summarized in Figure 10.1.

Even in the best of the situations outlined above, there will be somewhat limited access for students in a cooperative work group experience. However, there are two possible scenarios alluded to in Part I that can help alleviate these concerns:

- Using Internet access as a student variable in determining group composition

- Using online curricular material in the vertical files provided to the groups

Figure 10.1 Positive and Negative Aspects of School Computer Set-Up

Selected Setup	Positive Aspects	Negative Aspects
A computer lab	• Allows entire class to work together at one time • Provides students with access even if teacher is cyberphobic	• The larger the school, the more limited the access • Can take responsibility from teacher for integrating the lesson into the curriculum if cyberphobic
Classroom computer pods	• Allow significant computer access to students throughout the year • Teacher can do full classroom lessons with large display	• Limited number of classrooms and teachers can have the computers
Individual classroom computer	• All/most classrooms and teachers can have access to a computer • Teacher can do full classroom lessons with large display	• Significantly limited student access to one computer

As discussed in Part I, the teacher should determine which groups require Internet investigations, and then ensure that there is at least one student with Internet access at home in each of those groups. In an extended cooperative work group project, this will allow each group additional access to online material.

It was stated earlier in the chapter that one of the important characteristics of digital literacy is the integration of the information found online directly into the classroom curriculum. If Internet access for the students is significantly limited, then the teacher can locate relevant information on a home computer, print it, and duplicate the material for use in the vertical files that are provided for each group.[1] In this fashion, the students are still manipulating online material, and the URLs that are provided on the printed pages can lead to additional information or further research, as determined by the students.

Chapter 11 focuses on various effortless and efficient ways of locating this online curricular material.

PUTTING THEORY INTO PRACTICE: DETERMINING THE QUALITY AND QUANTITY OF INTERNET ACCESS

As part of his planning for the cooperative work group experience on helping the homeless, Mr. Washington had to determine the quantity and quality of Internet access for his students. He first conducted a private classroom survey of student Internet access. On a classroom test every two months throughout the year, he included the following question at the end of the exam:

Figure 10.2   Mr. Washington's Groups and Their Internet Needs

Group	Internet Needs
Drama	Required direct access
Music	Required online material supplied by drama group
Literature	Required online material supplied by drama group
Brochure Group, Investigation	Required direct access in addition to online material supplied by drama group
Brochure Group, Publication	No online access required

Do you have the Internet at home? Are you allowed to use it for classroom assignments?

Mr. Washington made a number of grouping decisions based on this information. First, he learned his students had limited Internet access (twelve of thirty-two students had it at home). In addition, he had no online access in his own classroom. However, there was access in the library resource center to which he could refer up to four students at a time. He also was allowed to send two or three students to the school's computer lab when other classes were present, if space permitted.

Using his students' online access, he determined that each of his cooperative work groups would fall into one of three categories:

- A group that needs direct Internet access for research.

- A group that needs material from the Internet; however, it does not have to be a product of their own investigation. They could work with material provided by other groups.

- A group that does not need online material.

Mr. Washington then assigned each group to one of the categories shown in Figure 10.2.

When guidelines for Internet access were established, Mr. Washington organized the following system with the students:

- The individual group would decide, in advance, exactly the type of information needed from the Internet to reduce search time on the computers.

- No more than two students from the Internet-using groups would go to the library and/or computer lab at one time.

- During the debriefing sessions, the status of the students' research would be shared among the groups. Those who were using online material accumulated from others (versus locating it on the Internet themselves) and who needed additional information, were able to share their needs. The Internet-using group, when time and opportunity was available, would locate the material during the following work session. If this was not feasible, two members from the group that required the material would be allowed to go online.

In this fashion, Mr. Washington was able to ensure that all of his cooperative work groups had sufficient access to Internet resources, while adapting to the limitations presented by the school's Internet access.

NOTE

1. Please note the copyright laws in your state. Most states have what is referred to as a "Fair Use" policy. This policy allows teachers to print material found on the Internet for classroom distribution only, as is described in this book.

How to Locate Curricular Material on the Internet

INTEGRATING THE INTERNET INTO THE CURRICULUM

A teacher is given a new novel to integrate into the English curricula. Though the teacher has never taught the particular book, she has a basic repertoire of teaching approaches. First, she knows how to teach novels—methodologies, projects, assessments, and so on. She also is innately aware of where to search, and not to, for additional material for that particular work. For example, it is doubtful she would go to an encyclopedia for supplemental materials on novels. Nor is it likely she would consult the classroom basal reader. However, through experience and prior education she would almost instinctively know where to turn in order to quickly and efficiently locate the supplement items necessary. The teacher has a degree of literacy in the area of English literature, which provides her with the direction as to where to proceed to acquire the necessary curricular materials.

Digital literacy operates under the same principles. It is the ability and knowledge to know what is available online, and where to acquire the necessary curricular materials. The most common teacher complaint is the extraordinary amount of time that it takes to locate items online. This problem is alleviated through the acquisition of digital literacy. The next section addresses the various types of places to which one can turn to quickly and efficiently locate any online curricular materials.

As emphasized in the previous chapter, digital literacy, as with all literacies, must begin with the teacher. Although all of the following strategies can easily be shared with the students, the teacher must first become proficient in their use.

Unfortunately, digital literacy is such a new topic that little research has been conducted in the area. The majority of educational articles on using the Internet have centered on either the basic concepts of digital literacy, or have presented specialized curricular activities developed by individuals.[1] In neither case are the basic principles of integrating the Internet into the curriculum offered in a general, widely applicable manner.

The Internet is evolving, especially regarding its use in education. The amount of curricular material available online is directly related to the subject area (see Mandel, 1999). There is a tremendous amount of material available on the Internet in the areas of History/Social Studies and the Language Arts. There is a growing amount of curricular material available in the Sciences, especially for biology and the earth sciences. However, there is a dearth of material in math, other than that used for statistical analysis (Dreir, Dawson, & Garofalo, 1997).

As stated in Chapter 5, the amount of material available for investigation will directly affect the outcomes of the cooperative work groups. In order for a teacher to ascertain whether or not online materials exist in a subject area, the teacher needs to learn how to efficiently and effectively use the Internet. These searching techniques—which ultimately will lead to the teacher's acquisition of digital literacy—can then be shared with the students as they begin the cooperative work group experience. The balance of this chapter explores in detail the various ways a teacher can locate this material.

There are five basic categories of Internet sites that provide good online curricular material.[2] Once a teacher has acquired a level of proficiency with these types of sites, searches for curriculum will become more productive, both in the quality and quantity of material that is acquired. The categories are

- Search engines and directories
- General education Web sites
- Comprehensive subject matter Web sites
- Specialty sites
- Teacher guest books

The following section is meant to serve as a basic "how to use" all of these types of sites in researching materials for cooperative work group experiences. Each of these subtopics has been divided into six subsections. The goal is to systematically and clearly assist the reader to achieve a personal level of digital literacy. Each area consists of

- A basic *description* of the types of Internet sites

- A narrative of the *basic functions* that the Internet sites provide the educator

- A discussion of *when these sites should be used* within the curricular planning process

- A discussion of the *special considerations* that need to be addressed when using these types of Internet sites

- An *example of how these Internet sites can be used* to acquire curricular material. Note that for the purposes of this discussion, all examples will come from two perspectives: a cooperative work group experience relating to the investigation of pioneer life in the late 1800s, and a science unit on life in the oceans.[3]

- An *exercise that the reader can experience* in order to become familiar with the variety of Internet sites

SEARCH ENGINES AND DIRECTORIES

Description

Search engines and directories are online tools that list thousands of Internet sites, providing the user with both a link and a short description of the Web page. These sites are similar to telephone-book yellow pages with one important exception—not every URL issued is automatically listed at these sites. Each has to be individually submitted by the Web site's author, and then accepted by the search engine or directory. As a result, there is no one online listing of all Internet addresses.

A search engine is different from a directory in that it simply lists all of the sites in its files alphabetically or by "key word." Search engines are also more accepting of Internet sites that are submitted to their files for inclusion.

Directories, on the other hand, list their files by category. They are also considerably more discriminating in the types of sites accepted into their database.

Basic Function

Both of these types of Internet sites are meant to provide numerous URLs on a particular topic. Both can access their files through use of a single "key word." With a directory, files can also be located through the subject categories that are displayed.

For example, in both search engines and directories, when a person types in the words "American Revolution" and clicks on the search button, the screen will soon display a list of Internet sites that contain the words "American Revolution" in either the title or somewhere within the site description. With a directory, links to the "American Revolution" also can theoretically be accessed through opening the "Countries" file, then the "United States" file, then the "History" file.

When These Sites Should Be Used

Search engines and directories should be used in two very specific situations:

- For initial curricular planning
- For locating a very specific Internet site

First, these tools should be used at the very beginning of curricular planning, when the teacher wants to find out "what is available." By doing a quick search on a topic in the initial stages of planning a unit or activity, the teacher can discern the basic quantity and quality of potential Internet sites to use.

Second, these sites should be used when looking for something very specific. For example, the teacher knows that there is a specific Internet site titled, "The Strange Mind of Edgar Allen Poe," but no longer has the URL. Use of a search engine or directory can immediately provide a link to that site (if, of course, the site is listed within one of their data banks).

Special Considerations

When using search engines and directories, there are a number of special considerations to be kept in mind.

Search engines are "dumb" sites. They do not know that the user is an educator, nor do they know exactly for what the teacher is searching. These sites simply provide the user with *everything* they have in their databases. This can become quite problematic. For example, using the search term "American Revolution" as noted above, LYCOS (one of the most well-known search engines) provides the reader with 924,649 listings of Internet sites that contain the words "American Revolution" either in their title or somewhere within their site description. This is obviously an unworkable list. If the teacher spent only one second scanning each description, it would still take approximately 257 hours to go through them all!

A solution to this problem is to use what is called a metasearch engine. This is a search engine with no database of its own. Rather, these sites search through all of the *other* major search engines, and list the top ten of each site (combining duplicates in the process). This makes the list much easier to manage. For example, using the term "American Revolution" with the metasearch engine METACRAWLER, the user is provided with only thirty-one links to Internet sites, which is a much more workable number.

It is also important to note that even though the number of sites is greatly reduced, the amount of pertinent information is not. For example, if the teacher was searching for material on the various battles of the American Revolution, there are probably thousands of references within the sites listed on Lycos. How much information does the teacher need? Fourteen of the sites provided on METACRAWLER contained some information on the various battles of the war. Chances are better than not that the teacher would find most, if not all, of the desired curricular material within those pages.

Another special consideration deals with directories. Directories, especially the most famous one, YAHOO!, contain fewer, but very reliable and useful sites. The operators of this site are extremely particular about the Internet pages they accept. In addition, most "official" and respectable sites from governments and municipalities can be located on this directory. YAHOO! is especially worthwhile when the teacher wants material of an "official" nature, such as anything having to do with a particular country, state, or municipality, or curricular information on famous individuals or topics.

Example of How These Internet Sites Can Be Used

Using the example of "Pioneer Life in the Late 1800s," the teacher wants to use a search engine to discover what types of sites are "available." Using METACRAWLER, the teacher types in the search term, "pioneer life," selects the "phrase" button (since it is more than one word), and then clicks on the search button. METACRAWLER then provides twenty Internet sites on this topic, including the following potentially useful locations[4]:

Conner Prairie Museum[5]. "Living history museum in Fishers, Indiana which also serves as a resource for research into 19th century pioneer life in the United States. Features a museum center, an 1836 village recreation, a house." http://connerprairie.org

Bonnyville and District Museum. "Offers exhibits of pioneer life in Alberta." http://collections.ic.gc.ca/bonnyville/English/historical_society.html

Pioneer & Frontier Life. "Collection titles: Pioneer and Frontier Life Letters, diaries, and other papers associated with exploration, the westward movement, overland travel, the gold rush, homesteading and settlement, and daily life on the frontier in the U.S." http://www.system.missouri.edu/whmc/pioneer.htm

Day in the Life. "Your class will delight in being pioneers for the morning or afternoon. Wake-up in The Log Cabin or Jury House, do chores and have a pioneer breakfast." http://www.pioneer.wwdc.com/educutn/daylife.htm

Pioneer Life. "Pioneer life in Connersville was tough. They had to work for themselves without modern conveniences or machines. When a pioneer came to Connersville, he had to make a clearing." http://fayette.k12.in.us/frazee/Pioneer_Life.html

Using METACRAWLER for the example of "Life in the Oceans," the teacher types in the search term, "ocean life," selects the "phrase" button (since it is more than one word), and then clicks on the search button. METACRAWLER then provides twenty-eight Internet sites on this topic, including the following potentially useful locations:

Cooluris, Jim. Seascapes, underwater scenes, marine life, and ocean monitoring. http://home.earthlink.net/~jcooluris

Institute of Marine Research. A Norwegian national center for research on coastal and ocean life and the marine environment. http://www.imr.no

Sustainable Seas Expeditions—Video Gallery. "Interactive Tour of the Monterey Bay National Marine Sanctuary 1998 Year of the Ocean Student Summit Monterey Bay Webcast Sustainable Seas Expeditions Channel Islands Webcast 1999 Education Highlights The McARTHUR Video Audio Only Video Video Take an . . ." http://sustainableseas.noaa.gov/aboutsse/media/media.html

Exercises That the Reader Can Experience

You are beginning to plan for a cooperative work group experience in which the students have to research and debate characteristics of democracy. You are not sure, however, whether there are sufficient materials online for your students to research to conduct a full investigation into this issue.

Go to METACRAWLER, and type in the search term "democracy." Look through the descriptions, and investigate some of the sites. Your goal is to determine whether or not enough curricular materials exist for this project through online resources.

GENERAL EDUCATION WEB SITES

Description

General education Web sites are Internet locations that offer a resource page containing numerous links to educational sites in all major curricular areas. Because these pages are sorted by subject, teachers can use them to immediately locate links to educational Internet sites.

Basic Function

The basic, primary function of a general education Web site is to make the teacher's life easier. These sites collect, analyze, and list the best educational Internet sites available today—rather than simply list *all* sites educational or not, as is the case with search engines and directories. Therefore, instead of researching various online sites to use as curricular resources, a teacher can go directly to a general education Web site and have this material immediately accessible, significantly reducing online search time.

When These Sites Should Be Used

After the initial "what is available" search, a general education Web site should be the first site used when beginning the process of curricular planning. These sites provide an immediate starting point for some of the best online resources to incorporate into the curricular project. What is more, depending on the general education Web site visited, the sites may immediately lead to additional Internet locations to research.

Special Considerations

There are two major general education Web sites, each with a slightly different focus: KATHY SCHROCK'S GUIDE FOR EDUCATORS and the Educational Resources page of TEACHERS HELPING TEACHERS. Both of these Internet resources are operated by teachers, and each site carefully analyzes and evaluates their listings for both educational content and teacher usefulness.

KATHY SCHROCK'S GUIDE FOR EDUCATORS is the more comprehensive of the two, listing hundreds of good educational sites in various categories. Regardless of their scope or subject matter, most good educational Internet locations will be listed on this site.

The Educational Resources page of TEACHERS HELPING TEACHERS is the more discriminating of the two. Rather than listing hundreds of sites, there are only a few dozen of the best Internet resources listed. In order for a site to be listed on this page it must pass three basic criteria:

• The site must be general in nature (i.e., there will not be a "Civil War" site listed, but there will be links to a number of excellent "history" sites).

• The site must contain a significant number of links to additional sites in that subject area, thereby allowing the teacher to easily investigate narrower topics.

• The site may not be a for-profit, commercial site.

Both sites are excellent to use when researching online curricular material. If time is an important factor, a teacher may locate something quicker from one of the sites on KATHY SCHROCK'S GUIDE FOR EDUCATORS. If the teacher has more time to fully investigate a topic, then TEACHERS HELPING TEACHERS will lead to subject matter sites that will, in turn, provide a great number of resources for curricular use.

Example of How These Internet Sites Can Be Used

In starting an online search for curricular materials on pioneer life in the late 1800s, the teacher initially chose "Educational Links" and then visited the

"Educational Resources" page of TEACHERS HELPING TEACHERS. In the "History/Social Studies" section, the teacher discovered the following potentially useful Internet links:

American Memory. "Collections of primary source and archival material relating to American culture and history from the Library of Congress"

EyeWitness. "Takes you to various historical events"

The Historical Text Archive. "Text of almost any major historical document you would want, especially American History"

The History Channel Web Site. "Primary source historical documentation, archives of great speeches and This Day In History section"

History/Social Studies Web Site for K-12 Teachers. "A hotlist of sources"

Women's History Home Page. "A guide to everything concerning women in history"

Starting an online search for curricular materials on ocean life, the teacher visited KATHY SCHROCK'S GUIDE FOR EDUCATORS. In the "Subject Access" section is a link to "Science and Technology." The teacher then selected the "Earth, Geology, & Oceanography" category, where the following potentially useful Internet links and descriptions were discovered:

Ancient Oceans. " . . . resources dealing with the paleontologic formation and the early marine life in the oceans"

Aquatic Habitats. " . . . a brief list of sites dealing with the ecology of the Chesapeake Bay and the Florida Everglades"

Aquatic Network. Resources. " . . . a well-compiled list of aquaculture, oceanography, and other marine-related sites"

Ocean Planet. " . . . a wonderful exhibit from the Smithsonian including pictures, information, and teacher materials about the ocean"

OceanLink. " . . . a link to marine science sites to support the grade 5–12 curriculum"

Exercise That the Reader Can Experience

You are planning a cooperative work group experience on human adaptations to different ecosystems (i.e., desert, rainforest, tundra, etc.). To start, you want to easily and quickly locate a number of good online educational sites that contain curricular material of various worldwide ecosystems (specifically, you are looking for descriptions, photographs, and information on human adaptations, plus animal and plant life).

Go to the Educational Resources page of TEACHING HELPING TEACHERS. Look through the various science listings and select a couple of links that would most likely lead you to useable sites. Take a look at the links you chose to ascertain whether they would be helpful to you or not.

COMPREHENSIVE SUBJECT MATTER WEB SITES

Description

The comprehensive subject matter Internet sites are very similar to those listed in the general education Web site section above. The primary difference is that these sites limit themselves to a comprehensive listing of Internet locations within one particular subject matter.

Basic Function

These online locations are also meant to make a teacher's life significantly easier. These are the key Internet sites for curricular research, and should be bookmarked for continual teacher use within specific subject areas. A comprehensive subject matter Web site should be immediately consulted whenever a teacher is searching for Internet resources.

When These Sites Should Be Used

These types of sites are the backbone of online curricular research. The majority of the time a teacher spends on the Internet searching for materials will be spent at sites such as these. A number of resources exist for each subject area, and the teacher will eventually decide which are the most useful.

Within the process of locating supplemental material for students, the teacher would find comprehensive subject matter Web sites through the use of the general education sites. The majority of the teacher's or students' research would then take place at these subject locations.

Special Considerations

Each curricular area has numerous comprehensive subject matter sites that are operated by an educational publisher, media company, university, other nonprofit educational entities, or an individual teacher. Each has its particular strengths and weaknesses.

In appearance, those operated by an educational publisher or media company are the most "professional." However, they often have limited sites available to the teacher. They link either to only those sites associated with their company, or to those that are generally very well known. Many good, teacher-developed Internet sites are not included on these lists.

The most useful of all of the comprehensive subject matter sites are those operated by universities or nonprofit educational entities. Being nonprofit, they are not beholden to any particular sites. In addition, these sites often include obscure, less well-known teacher sites that may have significant educational benefit.

The quality of Internet sites operated by individual teachers varies greatly. Sadly, many teachers are making their own "copycat" resource sites by rehashing many of the same links found throughout the Internet. The key to knowing if a private teacher's comprehensive subject matter site is worthwhile is twofold:

• How long has the site been established and operating? Sites older than two years are the most stable.

• Is the site considered good enough to be listed in the general education Web sites sited above?

Some of the best comprehensive subject matter Web sites include the following:

Language Arts
CHILDREN'S LITERATURE WEB GUIDE

Math
MATH FORUM

Social Studies
HISTORY/SOCIAL STUDIES WEB SITE FOR K-12 TEACHERS

Science
SCIENCE EDUCATION ZONE

The Arts
WORLD WIDE ARTS RESOURCE

Example of How These Internet Sites Can Be Used

Continuing the research on pioneer life in the 1800s, the teacher turns to the HISTORY/SOCIAL STUDIES WEB SITE FOR K-12 TEACHERS. The teacher selects "American History," then "Native Americans and the Frontier West." Links to more than two hundred sites are displayed on the screen, coupled with short descriptions. Among those sites are the following potentially appropriate links and descriptions for this unit:

National Museum of the American Indian. "What's New? | About the Museum | Exhibitions | Publications & Recordings Film & Video | Conexus | Calendar of Events & Activities | Education, Resources & Programs Membership & Development | Other Native American Sites | Research & Collections | Archive | About this Site"

Pioneering the Upper Midwest: Books from Michigan, Minnesota, and Wisconsin, ca. 1820–1910. "Offering first-person accounts, biographies, promotional literature, local histories, ethnographic and antiquarian texts, colonial archival documents, and other works drawn from the Library of Congress's General Collections and Rare Books and Special Collections Division. The 'Overview' section is a good place to start."

Frontier Culture Museum. "Can't think of a better place to start researching how various ethnic groups influenced the major occupation in American history—farming."

Images of the American West

Smithsonian Highlights. "Where the Prairie Grasses Grew."

The Northern Great Plains, 1880–1920. "(American Memory, Library of Congress)"

Continuing the research on ocean life, the teacher turns to the SCIENCE EDUCATION ZONE. The teacher selects "Links," then "Science Sites." A couple dozen sites are listed, most of which have links to additional sites. Among those sites are the following, each of which has numerous offerings for the Ocean Life unit:

Science Sites. More links than you can shake a stick at!

Amateur Science. Lots of fun projects and links.

Franklin Institute Online Science Museum

Exercise That the Reader Can Experience

You are gathering resources for a cooperative work group experience on life in Roman times. Using the following three comprehensive subject matter sites, locate resource material for your project:

HISTORY/SOCIAL STUDIES WEB SITE FOR K-12 TEACHERS. Use this site to locate information about life at this time

CHILDREN'S LITERATURE WEB GUIDE. Use this site to locate ancient Roman literature, including mythological stories

WORLD WIDE ARTS RESOURCE. Use this site to locate examples of Roman art and architecture

SPECIALTY SITES

Description

Specialty sites are the foundation of the Internet. These are all of the locations that exist for one particular topic. The sites may cover a broad area, such as the Civil War; or may have an extremely narrow focus, such as the online site on Mongolian music. Either way, virtually all of the curricular information a teacher will use from the Internet will come from specialty sites. These are most easily located through the use of general education and comprehensive subject matter Web sites.

Basic Function

The basic function of specialty sites is to provide the reader with information and pictures on a given topic. For both the teacher and student, this is where the vast majority of online curricular material and information will be located.

When These Sites Should Be Used

The entire goal of the process of searching for material on the Internet is to ultimately locate specialty sites, quickly and efficiently. These are the Internet locations that contain the information and material that will be collected and used. It is the process of locating these sites that consumes the vast majority of a teacher's online time. Digital literacy occurs when the teacher instinctively knows when these types of online resources exist, how to locate them, and how to incorporate the material into the curriculum.

Special Considerations

There is little control over either the quality or the authoritativeness of specialty sites. Teachers need to use their own repertoires of already-acquired skills for the evaluation of educational materials. For example, when a teacher visits an educational bookstore and picks up a new item, she or he naturally evaluates the material through various filters acquired via years of experience in the educational field. The same process is used in evaluating specialty sites. It is imperative that the following be part of one's evaluation of Internet sites for potential use within the curricula:

- Is the information accurate?

- Does the information have a perceptible slant or point of view?

- Who authors the sites? Is it an organization (educational or commercial), or an individual? If it is an individual, is the person identified? Does the site provide an e-mail address to contact the author?

- Is the information useful, or does more and better material exist on another site previously located?

- When was the site last updated?

Using the answers to the above questions—both positive and negative—the teacher then needs to determine the overall value of the site to the curriculum. "Questionable" sites may still prove to be valuable for teacher research or for acquiring materials for the cooperative work group vertical files. Pictures or written material may be appropriate if taken out of the original context of the site. For example, pictures of medieval castles may still prove to be valuable for the lesson, even though they come from a "religious" site, not normally acceptable for student use. The teacher would simply print or copy and paste the picture, and use it as a valuable curricular resource.

It is the *information* that is provided on the site that determines a specialty site's importance, *not the specific site itself.* This is critical because teachers typically keep lists of sites to visit or purchase books of Internet "Yellow Pages." These collected sites not only may not contain the specific material needed for the particular curricular topic, but the URL may not even work by the time the teacher attempts to use it. For these reasons, the process outlined above is necessary in order to locate supplemental sites in a particular subject area.

For example, a teacher needing information on Egyptian pyramids was provided with an Internet site on ancient Egypt. Unfortunately, three months later when the teacher tried the URL, it no longer worked. The teacher must know there are hundreds, possibly thousands, of other sites online that contain this kind of information.

Figure 11.1   Use of Specialty Sites for Cooperative Work Group Experience on Pioneer Life in the Late 1800s

Title of Internet Site	Basic Use of the Site
The Food Timeline	Recipes for dishes developed at various historical times, using ingredients available in stores today.
Frontier Culture Museum	Numerous examples of various facets of frontier culture. Great graphics.
Bibliography of North American Indians	Direct links to information on any of the Native American tribes that lived in the area and time of the pioneers
The Northern Great Plains: 1880–1920	Many pictures of life in the northern Great Plains with a searchable subject index
The Old-Timers Page	Fun cultural explanations of how to do things such as making soap, potting meat and knowing where to dig a well.

By using general education and comprehensive subject matter Web sites, the teacher can locate alternate resources in just minutes. It now is irrelevant whether the teacher used that particular site. What is important is that the required material could be located somewhere else on the Internet.

Example of How These Internet Sites Can Be Used

Through the use of the general education and comprehensive subject matter sites, the teachers in the pioneer example (see Figure 11.1) and the ocean life example (see Figure 11.2) located online resources that provided critical curricular information for the cooperative work group experiences.[6]

Exercise That the Reader Can Experience

You are putting together vertical files for a cooperative work group experience for a unit on "American Culture in the 60s." Locate and review the following specialty sites to determine what material from each site would be beneficial to include in the vertical files for the students (for this particular application, the URLs have been included for ease of use):

Psychedelic '60s: Home Page. www.lib.virginia.edu/exhibits/sixties/index.html

We Shall Overcome; Historic Places of the Civil Rights Movement National Register Travel Itinerary. www.cr.nps.gov/nr/travel/civilrights

Figure 11.2 Use of Specialty Sites for Cooperative Work Group Experience on Ocean Life

Title of Internet Site	Basic Use of the Site
Kids Corner International Year of the Ocean	Tremendous number of links on these topics: Fish and Ocean Critters; The Ocean; Teacher Goodies; Sea Grant; Environmental Programs; Weather and Climate; Coast and Estuaries; History; Ships
Ocean Collection for Kids	This is a collection of sites that have ocean-related topics.
Free Ocean Life Pictures!	Screensaver pictures of ocean life to use during the unit
Welcome to Life in The Ocean	Great teaching tool—online lessons

The Vietnam War: A Teacher's Resource. www.tappedin.org/info/teachers/vietnam1.htm

The Trial of the Chicago Seven. www.law.umkc.edu/faculty/projects/ftrials/Chicago7/chicago7.html

TEACHER GUEST BOOKS

Description

Teacher guest books are similar to online "bulletin boards" in that teachers can post questions, make requests, and provide answers for other teachers nationally and internationally. The difference between bulletin boards and guest books, however, is that a guest book is more personal and private. Whereas a teacher can always post an answer directly on a bulletin board, on a guest book, the teacher has the opportunity to personally send the requestors an e-mail, since their e-mail address is linked to their message. This presents two very important benefits of guest books over bulletin boards:

• Teachers who may not want their answers viewed publicly are more apt to send them in an e-mail than to post them on a bulletin board.

• Teachers who read a message on a guest book do not know if it has already been answered, and therefore are more apt to respond. Consequently, a teacher who posts a question on a guest book may receive a variety of answers rather than only one or two publicly posted on the bulletin board.

Basic Function

The basic function of teacher guest books is to allow for teacher networking. A guest book allows the teacher to ask a question, request materials, or simply bond with others in the profession.

Guest books are extremely easy to use. One of the most popular teacher guest books is on the Internet site TEACHERS HELPING TEACHERS. Once a teacher clicks on the link to the guest book, he or she can interact with the other readers in one of two ways:

- *Add a message.* Click on the link marked "Add." The user will be immediately provided with a form to fill in one's name, city, state, country, and e-mail address. (An element of privacy is assured for there is no place for a snail-mail address or a phone number). A large box is then provided in which the message to be displayed can be typed. Once the "submit" button is clicked, the message is posted.

- *Respond to someone's message.* Click on the e-mail address of that teacher. An e-mail form will appear automatically addressed to that person. The form is then completed and sent, as is done with any e-mail.

With a guest book, teachers can scroll through the list of messages and respond only to those they find interesting or relevant to their teaching and interests. With this particular guest book, those who post questions and requests typically receive three to twelve responses within forty-eight hours.

When These Sites Should Be Used

In two specific instances, a teacher guest book should be used in the planning process:

- When the teacher cannot locate a resource or has come to an impasse. A request for information can often produce unexpected answers or hard-to-locate materials.

- When the teacher wants a new, fresh perspective on teaching in a curricular area, and requests ideas others may wish to share.

Special Considerations

There are no special considerations for using a teacher guest book. The process is straightforward. It is important to be direct. Do not go into lengthy detail about one's teaching situation or students unless it is germane to the question. A great many teachers scan through the guest book listings. A short direct question or statement, such as, "I'm looking for some good Web sites on the works of Robert Frost. Any suggestions?" will lead to many more responses than a long paragraph explaining the overall unit and classroom environment.

Another suggestion is that the teacher looking for specific information should scan the guest book for others who teach the same subject or grade level and send them an e-mail, asking what they have experienced in the requested curricular area.

Example of How These Internet Sites Can Be Used

The teacher in the pioneering unit example could not locate Internet sites with curricular material for some specific subject areas. After an extensive search, she placed this e-mail on a teacher guest book:

> I cannot find any Web sites with information on plants and animals of the northern Great Plains in the late 1800s, nor of how soddies were actually constructed (I have pictures of soddies but not explanations of how they were built). Any suggestions?

Within forty-eight hours, she received six responses, including the following:

> *Lincoln, Nebraska.*[7] We had a Western Cultural Arts Day to teach our students here in Nebraska more about their past. The following Web addresses were given to the teachers for resources. They may be helpful in what you are looking for: www.bbps.k12.ne.us/custer/academics/sodhouse/interview. htm Nebraska pioneers; hollis.peoria.k12.il.us/students/mic/index~1.htm; www.websteader.com/wbstdsd1.htm this one is specifically about pioneer sod houses; www.rootsweb.com/~neresour/OLLibrary/Journals/HPR/ index.html this one is an index and a link to many Nebraska pioneer history sites
>
> Most were built into a cliff side. The sod was cut into bricklike shapes and placed like slump blocks. I will try to get you more documentation. Smithsonian magazine and Scientific American as well as National Geographic are good links.

> *Chicago, Illinois.* I will get back to you on this although I have more info on Az and Hopi plants, etc.

The teacher in the ocean life unit example also could not locate Internet sites with curricular material for some specific subject areas. As a result, she placed this e-mail on a teacher guest book:

> I cannot find any Web sites with information on the various ocean life found in kelp beds. Any suggestions?

Within forty-eight hours, she received five messages, including the following:

> *New Orleans, Louisiana.* There are some great pictures of kelp beds at: http://www.gygis.com and at http://life.bio.sunysb.edu/marinebio/ kelpforest.html.

> *San Jose, California.* Have you looked at the Monterey Bay Aquarium site? They should have some pictures there.

> *Washington, D.C.* PBS had a special on the ocean. I think it was called Secrets of the Ocean. Their stuff is usually online when they have a special. I don't have the URL, but I think it's pbs.com. Take a look for it.

Exercise That the Reader Can Experience

Go to the guest book of TEACHERS HELPING TEACHERS. Select a unit or lesson that you are currently planning, and post a request for information concerning some aspect of it. You can ask for Internet sites, curricular materials, or ideas from fellow teachers.

Attaining digital literacy is the ultimate goal of working with the Internet in education. Digital literacy involves the innate knowledge of what curricular materials exist on the Internet, how to quickly and efficiently access those materials, and how to seamlessly integrate them into any given curricula. Through the knowledge and correct use of search engines and directories, general education Web sites, comprehensive subject matter sites, specialty sites, and teacher guest books, a teacher can obtain, through practice, advanced skills in the first two areas of digital literacy. The third area—how to seamlessly integrate the online material into the curriculum—is the focus of the next chapter.

PUTTING THEORY INTO PRACTICE: FINDING INTERNET RESOURCES FOR STUDENTS

During the planning of his cooperative work group experience, Mr. Washington did his own investigation of potential Internet sites for the students to use. Initially, he imagined that he would eventually do the vast majority of the research, and then place the curricular material into vertical files. However, as he worked his way through the sites,

Box 11.1

Tips for Keeping Your Sanity and Saving Time While Working With the Internet

The Internet will test your sanity through continued use. Web sites sometimes take an extraordinary amount of time to download; often a site that was visited recently will suddenly not work—virtually disappearing into cyberspace. This can become extremely frustrating when doing research.

Before panic sets in, or "violence" is directed toward the computer, follow these steps when a site you want is no longer in operation:

1. *Check out the letters, numbers, and symbols of the URL, if you typed it in yourself.* Computers are "dumb" machines. They cannot read minds. Even one incorrect punctuation mark in a URL will prevent you from connecting with that Internet site.

2. *Wait a day or two, if you have the time, and attempt the site again.* The Internet uses a convoluted route through phone and cable lines to get to your computer. A thunderstorm in Atlanta can easily knock out service in Los Angeles.

3. *Go backwards through the URL to the original home page.* Very often, a URL will contain "files" to specific pages that are linked to the home page. These links may be changed, be renamed, or may disappear, but the home page could still be functioning. Take the following fictional URL as an example:

www.Americanrevolution.org/washington/delawareriver

This URL points to a file about the "Delaware River" contained within a larger file titled "Washington." That file is subsequently found on the www.Americanrevolution.org Web site. However, if this page seems to no longer exist, go back one level to the "Washington" page and type in:

www.Americanrevolution.org/washington

Reference to the desired material may be located elsewhere on this page. However, if this page does not work either, go back one more level to the home page:

www.Americanrevolution.org

Box 11.1 Continued

Many times the information may be linked in a new way to the home page. By going backwards, you have the opportunity to methodically search the primary source of the site. However, if the main page URL does not work either, it is time to go to the next step.

4. *Try a search for the missing Internet site.* Individuals or organizations that operate Web sites change servers, or simply decide on a different URL. The original site may still exist, but the address is no longer valid. In these cases, check if a new URL has been established and listed. Go to a metasearch engine such as METACRAWLER and type in the name of the site. If the site still exists (and has been listed on any major search engine), you will be provided with a link to the new URL. If not, there's one last step to use.

5. *Search for a new Internet site with the same information.* As stated earlier, information is duplicated throughout the Internet. If you are looking for a specific or general topic, use the steps outlined throughout this chapter to find new online material: search engines and directories, general education Web sites, comprehensive subject matter Web sites, specialty sites, and teacher guest books. You are sure to locate what you want through the use of one of these tools. For example, using the fictional example in 3, if you wanted information on "Washington crossing the Delaware River" and that URL no longer was working, you would probably find similar, appropriate material in the American History section of the comprehensive subject matter Internet site HISTORY/SOCIAL STUDIES WEB SITE FOR K-12 TEACHERS.

By following these five procedures, you can save tremendous stress when working with the peculiarities of the Internet. Remember that this is a new and growing technology, using resources (e.g., telephone lines) that were never meant for this purpose. Web sites come and go with regularity. Learning how to deal with this phenomenon is crucial for successfully integrating the Internet into your curriculum, and ultimately achieving digital literacy.

and subsequently discovered that some of the groups would have sufficient online access within the school, he decided that the students could easily locate much of the material on their own, with some guidance on his part.

Mr. Washington first visited the search engine METACRAWLER in order to ascertain "what was out there." Using the search term "homeless," he received twenty-nine different links to sites. Although the majority of them pertained to efforts in specific cities, a number were general resources, including the following useable sources:

Coalition for the Homeless. "The National Coalition for the Homeless is a national advocacy network of homeless persons, activists, service providers, and others committed to . . .

Are the Homeless to Blame? "Robust debate about this and other hot issues on TheFence.com, the Internet's premier debate community . . . 300 articles, from politics to pop culture. Which side of The Fence are you on? www.thefence.com (GoTo.com)"

Mr. Washington then decided to look at a general education Web site to determine if there were any useable educational Internet locations available. He knew that the Educational Resources page of TEACHERS HELPING TEACHERS had a section on Social Action. Although he found no comprehensive subject matter sites for this particular subject area, he did discover the following helpful specialty sites:

The Hunger Site. Donate food for free to hungry people around the world

54 Ways You Can Help the Homeless

VolunteerMatch. Dedicated to using the power of the Internet to find volunteers for nonprofit, community based organizations and causes

Finally, Mr. Washington took one last glance through the social studies comprehensive subject matter site, the HISTORY/SOCIAL STUDIES WEB SITE FOR K-12 TEACHERS. Under the "Current Issues in the News" section he found a number of potentially useful listings:

The Forgotten Fourteen Million: The Politics of Poverty (News Feature). "A Coproduction with National Public Radio SM Stories: Falling Behind in Kentucky, Schooling Poor Kids in Minneapolis, Children in the Fields, The Politics of Child Poverty. RealAudio 3.0 needed to listen."

Public Agenda, Public Agenda Online: Public Policy Research. "Looks at the current issues of: Abortion, America's Global Role, Crime, The Economy, Education, The Environment, The Family, The Federal Budget, Gambling, Health Care, Illegal Drugs, Immigration, Internet Speech/Privacy, Medicare, Race, Right to Die, Social Security, Welfare. Each issue is examined in a broad objective framework with a variety of opinions and views on the issue."

Census Article on Poverty

Child Poverty News. Series on Welfare Reform from a Children's Perspective.

Once he acquired this list of Internet sites, Mr. Washington listed them on paper and made them available to the students. Since his main goal was primarily curricular in nature, versus teaching online research skills, this allowed the students to save time searching for appropriate sites, and ultimately provide more time for working with the information provided by the online material.

As one last attempt to acquire additional ideas for this experience, Mr. Washington placed the following message on the teacher guest book of TEACHERS HELPING TEACHERS:

My students are developing a program for their classmates to help the homeless in our town. Does anyone have any suggestions on information for this project or ideas that they can share with others?

Within two days, he received nine responses, including the following:

Los Angeles, California. There is a newspaper actually put out by the homeless in Santa Monica. They have a link on the web, but I don't know it. Do a Yahoo search under Santa Monica, I'm pretty sure that it's there.

St. Louis, Missouri. Take a look at Homeless.com—www.rightwhale.org. Lots of good stuff there.

New York, New York. Have the students each experience social action themselves by going to a food bank one morning or volunteering at some location in your town. Then they can share their experiences.

NOTES

1. As examples, see two issues of *Educational Leadership* that were devoted to technology: Volume 55, No. 3, "Integrating Technology into Teaching," and Volume 56, No. 5, "Integrating Technology into the Curriculum."

2. Please note that this is a very basic list for Internet novices. More specialized sites, such as listservs, gophers, and so on, are not dealt with in this text. These are useful tools that one readily discovers after acquiring a degree of digital literacy.

3. As with the other material in this chapter, all URLs to the sites listed in these examples are included in Resource A. The exception to this rule is when the text quotes a list of links from another online source as an example of the types of sites that are available.

4. Please note that whenever a list of sites is quoted from either a database, search engine, or other Internet resource, it will be printed here *exactly* as it appears on the original site. Their URLs will not be included in Resource A, however, because they are not germane to the discussion. Rather, they serve only as examples of the types of resources that are available at a particular Internet site.

5. Italicized lettering in a quoted example denotes a direct link to that particular site.

6. Many of the sites listed in the earlier comprehensive subject matter example are considered "specialty sites." However, to avoid repetition, none of the previously listed sites are included in either this figure or Figure 11.2.

7. For privacy reasons, only the location of the e-mail sender has been included.

Integrating the Internet Into Cooperative Work Group Experiences

DETERMINING THE BEST USE OF ONLINE RESOURCES

With cooperative work group experiences, most of the integration of Internet resources into the curriculum comes in the form of supplying curricular material for student use through the vertical file system. The quality and quantity of student online access is the ultimate determining factor. Some teaching situations allow the students to use this technology within the assigned group work time, either in the classroom or through the use of other computers in the school. In both of these scenarios, the teacher, or the students, should follow the procedures outlined in the previous section:

- Decide the types of material required

- Determine the current stage of the planning and investigation process

- Settle on the most efficient means of locating the required curricula online

Once the teacher and the students become fully involved with this process, once they acquire a working familiarity with the various types of useful, accessible Internet sites available, they will all begin to acquire true digital literacy.

The key to all of this is *practice*. Practice helps acquire a working familiarity, with online resources becoming a natural part of one's cognitive repertoire. Practice permits the teachers and the students to instinctively know *what* is available and *where* it is available through online resources.

For example, if a student work group wants a copy of the Magna Carta for some point of their project research, they—and the teacher—should know that one could probably be found on the HISTORICAL TEXT ARCHIVE site, and that they could probably find a link to that location through either TEACHERS HELPING TEACHERS or KATHY SCHROCK'S GUIDE FOR EDUCATORS. All involved have acquired a measure of digital literacy when they innately arrive at that knowledge.

However, there still are a number of practical, everyday issues to be addressed in order to efficiently and successfully integrate the Internet into cooperative work group experiences. These include the following:

- Knowing when to use, or not use, technology

- How to integrate online material when there is no school access to the Internet

- Parental issues: Security concerns and public relations

KNOWING WHEN TO USE, OR NOT USE, TECHNOLOGY

A news radio station in Los Angeles recently conducted a survey of its listeners as to their buying habits on the Internet. Internet shopping has been a recent phenomenon in California—from household items, to groceries, to cars, to home loans—and there is an extremely high number of computers in people's homes. However, much to its surprise, the station discovered that less than one third of those who shop for a car on the Internet actually purchase it online. They found that the vast majority of people still preferred to see the car in person before purchase. Contrary to their beliefs, they discovered that because people *could* make a purchase on the Internet, did not mean that they *would*.

The Internet is in a similar situation in the educational world. Whereas one can locate virtually any curricular material online—it may not be efficient to use it as such. This is part of digital literacy: knowing when to find curricular items online, and when not to use the technology.

Often in research, an encyclopedia, book, or other resource may provide the required material faster and easier than searching for an online source. Sometimes the Internet may be a better choice. The answer comes from a balance of knowing exactly what one is looking for, the various places to find it, and the amount of time and energy necessary to complete the task. Learning how *not* to waste time is a key skill that leads to success in the business world. Figure 12.1 gives a number of practical examples taken from typical cooperative work group tasks.

The common thread through all of these examples is that if the resource already exists at the school site, and it is reasonably accessible, use the school resource. The Internet should not be incorporated as a research tool just because it's there. Remember, the ultimate goal of student research is to acquire the resources needed to achieve the project goal. If resources can be located through quicker, ordinary, "nonelectronic" means, so much the better.

HOW TO INTEGRATE ONLINE MATERIAL EVEN WHEN THERE IS NO SCHOOL ACCESS TO THE INTERNET

Quality and quantity of student online access is a significant variable in the planning and coordination of cooperative work group experiences. Obviously, the most current problem for the teacher is when there is no Internet access at the school. Even when access is available at the school, students may not be able to use the resource

Figure 12.1   Some Examples of When to Use the Internet, When Not to Use It

When the students want to locate . . .	They should not use the Internet when they need . . .	They should use the Internet when they need . . .
A map	A modern map that would be easily located in an encyclopedia or historical/modern atlas	A specialty map that would not be normally accessible from, or postdates these sources
A well-known document	Something that is readily available in a classroom text—such as the Declaration of Independence	A more obscure resource or one from a foreign culture
Material about a country, famous personality or event, or a local resource	Basic facts about something they are researching—they can probably find the material quicker through the use of an encyclopedia, book, or if it is a local entity, a phone call	Deeper or more obscure material, especially in the case of cultural information
A piece of literature	A well-known piece of literature that could be located through normal school on-site resources	A piece of literature that is more obscure or cannot be found easily on the school site.
Pictures	Pictures that are know to exist within a classroom or library resource	Pictures that they do not immediately know where to turn in order to locate the resource

due to scheduling conflicts with other classes, or as is sometimes the case, the system is down. Still, there are a number of ways that a teacher can cope with this challenging condition.

First, in situations where the school is wired to the Internet but access happens to be unavailable during the research time, the teacher must remember that cooperative work group experiences last more than one or two class sessions. They are longer-term projects. Therefore, if the Internet is down one or two days, or access is not obtainable, there are other workdays when the students can use the online resources. This is an important discussion topic for the debriefing sessions with the students—"what if" there is no online access the following day? What will the groups accomplish? Will they still be able to work? What advanced planning will be needed? This provides an opportunity for advanced, higher-level thinking processes where the students will need to analyze their tasks, synthesize the material they have and that they will need for their tasks, and to evaluate their status.

Although the teaching situation is significantly different when the school is not wired to the Internet, successful cooperative work group experiences can still result with advanced planning. When the teacher knows that no access is available, the teacher has two alternatives:

- Plan for the "rule of one third" when formulating the cooperative work groups
- Make extensive use of vertical files

The "rule of one third" was introduced in Part I regarding using Internet access as a student variable in the formulation of the cooperative work groups. If at least one third of the class has online access at home, then there are enough students to incorporate its use as a requirement in cooperative work group projects. (One third is used as the threshold so there will be enough students with home access so that individuals will not be singled out as a socioeconomic "have" versus the "have-nots.") When formulating groups, the teacher simply ensures that for every group that requires online access for its research, at least one or two students with Internet access at home are assigned to that unit (see Figure 2.4 for a practical example of this process).

Probably the easiest and most efficient way to have the students incorporate material from online resources when student access does not exist is through the use of the vertical file system (described in full in Chapter 4). In this scenario, the teacher personally acquires the online material at home, prints it out, copies it if necessary, and then places the pages in their appropriate vertical files for the students to use in their research. In this situation it is not important whether or not the students locate the materials themselves, but that they have access to the wealth of data from the online resources.

For example, using the earlier pioneering unit: If the teacher did not have Internet access for the students, pages of types of transportation, housing, culture, and so on, could have been printed from their Internet sources, duplicated, and placed into vertical files for those students to use. Although the students would not have accessed the material *personally*, they would still have the data at their disposal to analyze, evaluate, and synthesize into their final project.

The teacher can also call on parents at the beginning of a new unit to help locating online resources in a particular curricular area. For example, the teacher of the pioneering unit might have sent home the following request a week or two prior to the start of the cooperative work group experience:

Dear Parents:

We are beginning a new unit on pioneer life on the Great Plains in the late 1800s. This unit will include a cooperative work group project where the students will simulate a "County Fair" exemplifying life and culture at this time.

Since we have limited Internet access at school, it would be helpful if our parents did some investigating at home, and sent in good curricular materials that they might locate online. The students can then use these materials as resources throughout their investigations.

We are looking for:

- Examples of life and culture during that time

- Examples of housing, transportation, food, the land, and Native American tribes that the pioneers would have encountered

For all of these sites, please send only pages that contain pictures with explanations. Also, please make sure that the URL is located somewhere on that page.

Thank you for your help with providing our students with the most modern, up-to-date educational materials to use in their investigations.

The parents of those students would then provide many pages of potentially useful curricular material. The teacher would sort the submissions and decide which to discard and which were of value. The end result is that with the incorporation of the vertical file system, the students would integrate relevant, modern online materials into their cooperative work group experience even though they did not have direct access to the Internet.

Please note that having the parents conduct initial searches is different from students' searching for material. The parents are providing core resources that are then used by the students in their cooperative work groups. Normally, at this early stage of the unit, the students would not have enough knowledge of the subject matter to know what to look for during an online search, nor would they be able to evaluate the worth of the curricular material.

PARENTAL ISSUES: SECURITY CONCERNS AND PUBLIC RELATIONS

Security Concerns

Security is one of the most prevalent concerns of parents, administrators, and teachers toward student Internet access. In basic terms, how does one prevent the students from having access to inappropriate sites. It is an important enough concern to having kept students off of the Internet. Unfortunately, this also prevents students from gaining the substantial educational advantages of using the Internet and from acquiring the digital literacy that will be required of people in the twenty-first–century workplace.

Regretfully, the media have significantly exaggerated this problem. The inappropriate sites that the students are most likely to access are those of their favorite music, television, or movie stars, or those of their personal interests, such as pro wrestling. These are the online, off-task behaviors that will most likely confront the teacher, not sexually explicit sites.

The majority of these problems will be alleviated through simple, good classroom management skills. If the teacher is aware of what the students are doing, and if the students know the consequences of inappropriate actions, then most problems can be avoided.

For example, if the groups are working on research concerning ancient Egypt, and the teacher notices two students laughing and pointing at their computer screen, they had better be looking at a Web site featuring ancient Egyptian comedians. Otherwise, they could loose their computer privileges as a consequence. If the teacher goes over to their computer and sees an "approved" site on the screen, use of the browser "back" button can immediately display what the students were originally laughing at. This is simple classroom management:

• The students and parents know what is expected of the students while on the Internet

• The students and parents are aware of the positive and negative consequences of student actions

• The teacher actively monitors their progress

In addition, for both legal and public relations concerns with the parents, an "Acceptable-Use Policy" type of "contract" can be signed by all students prior to allowing them Internet access within the school. An example of such a form is included in Resource C. This is a working document used at one large urban middle school, and may be reproduced for use by the reader. Note: Because this is a document for parents, have it translated into the major language groups at your site.

Security software is easily accessible and relatively inexpensive. These are programs that prevent students from accessing certain Internet sites that contain specific "unacceptable" words. Be aware, however, of three potential problems with this software:

• The software is not foolproof. Internet-savvy secondary school students can usually find ways around it if they so desire.

• The software blocks out many legitimate sites—especially in the science and health field—because it does not search for inappropriate content, but rather, it looks for specific key words.

• Security software also tends to cause problems with other software on the computer and may lead to system crashes and other technological headaches.

Again, rather than relying on security software, good classroom management skills along with written agreements among the school, student, and parents can prevent most potential problems.

The same type of answer should be shared with parents who express concern over allowing their child online access at home. Good parenting skills—for example, monitoring what their children are doing—can and should address these security concerns. Internet security at home is a parenting issue, not a school curricular issue.

Public Relations

The easiest way for the teacher to gain the support and encouragement of parents is through good public relations work. Parents who question students' working online generally fall into two very different categories:

- Those who want their children to become proficient with the Internet

- Those who are afraid of what their children will be exposed to on the Internet

The answer to both types of parents is relatively simple and involves good public relations efforts on behalf of the school.

The parents who desire that their children become proficient on the Internet generally will voice concern that the students are not working with online sources enough. They are fretful that there is not sufficient student access in the school or the classroom. One of the answers to these parents is the creation of a "newsletter" at the beginning of new units or lessons. This document provides the parents with specific URLs that they can personally access in order to see the types of sites that are being incorporated into the curricula. This also gives the parents an opportunity to personally assist their children in supplementing and understanding the curricular material that is being discussed within the classroom. Either way, the parents can learn that their children's teacher has a degree of digital literacy, and that their youngster is benefiting from the teacher's knowledge of Internet resources.

The parents who are afraid of what their children will be exposed to on the Internet generally do not know or understand the benefits of this technology to the school curricula. These are parents who most likely do not have Internet access at home, and have been influenced by negative media portrayals of the Internet as a tool to lure children into dangerous situations. The answer to these parents is through adult education. For example, have a "parent workshop" where the teacher demonstrates to the parents the benefits of the Internet, how it operates, how it is integrated into the curriculum, and how their security concerns are addressed. In this fashion, the teacher not only alleviates their legitimate fears, but also provides positive public relations for the classroom program, helping the parents to "buy into" what is being taught.

It is important to remember that the more the parents support and assist the classroom curricula concerning use of the Internet, the easier it will be for the teacher, and the better the educational experiences will be for the students.

PUTTING THEORY INTO PRACTICE: DEALING WITH THE LAST ISSUES

Mr. Washington was just about finished with his planning of the cooperative work group experience. He had just a few more areas to investigate in the use of Internet resources.

Mr. Washington wanted his students to realize when it would be efficient to use online resources, and when to use other resources. In a classroom discussion, he created a research chart on the board. The students discussed the types of online materials they required. They then discussed whether using an Internet source or other source would be the most efficient. The class arrived at the conclusions shown in Figure 12.2.

Figure 12.2   Chart for Mr. Washington's Class For When to Use Online Resources and When Not to Use Them

Topic Area	Internet Use?	Other Media Use?
Data about the homeless	Yes	Yes, as a supplement for hometown agencies—use brochures and local publications
Anecdotes about the lives of the homeless	Yes	No, other than comic relief video
Hometown opportunities to help the homeless	No	Yes, use Yellow Pages to locate local help agencies and get pertinent information

The issue of Internet access was not a significant problem for Mr. Washington. Knowing his students' online access would be somewhat limited, he determined how many, and which groups, would need to actively do online research. He configured the groups' composition so every group that needed to use the Internet had one or more students with online access at home. In addition, he arranged for both the school library resource center and the computer lab to allow a limited number of students to use the Internet when needed. This advanced planning ensured him that there would be sufficient online access for a successful cooperative work group project.

Inappropriate sites were also not a major concern for Mr. Washington, although it was an issue he had to specifically address with this particular topic. His students had had experience working on the Internet and knew what was expected of them, and the negative consequences if they visited inappropriate sites. However, the problems of the homeless were sometimes "grouped" with other society issues involving AIDS, and ultimately sexual issues and topics. He thus led a whole class discussion about what they should do if they accidentally opened an inappropriate site. This was a potential problem since the district's security firewall would not screen all objectionable material. Therefore, the students were directed, if they opened an objectionable site, to do the following:

- Immediately click on the "back" button to leave the site

- If there was other usable material on the site that the students wanted to incorporate into their research, they were to inform Mr. Washington, who would then access the specific data.

The students were informed that if these procedures were not followed, they would lose their school Internet privileges.

Public relations was not an issue for Mr. Washington, for he kept the parents informed of the project from the very beginning. The parents saw the educational value of the project, and were aware of the higher-order thinking skills that were being practiced. In the end, when they observed the final project—the brochure and the assembly, which they were invited to attend—they all agreed that this cooperative work group project on the plight of the homeless was an extremely worthwhile educational endeavor.

A FINAL NOTE

Digital literacy becomes an important component for students being prepared for the work place of the twenty-first century. Students, and their teachers, need to know how to efficiently and easily integrate the powers of the Internet into the various curricula of the school. In order to achieve this goal, the teacher needs to deal with a number of issues and situations. First, the teacher needs to understand how the quality and quantity of student access to online resources directly affects the specific curricula of the classroom, especially in cooperative work group experiences. Second, the teacher needs to be comfortable with and knowledgeable about the various types of Internet sites that exist, and be able to "instinctively" know how to locate any type of material that may be beneficial to the curricular goals. Finally, the teacher needs to be aware of how to practically integrate the powers of the Internet into the curriculum, when and when not to use it, plus address concerns of security and public relations.

The end result of this entire process is true digital literacy for the teacher and ultimately the students—a digital literacy that will allow the students to effortlessly integrate this modern technology into their lives and education, better preparing them for a successful career in twenty-first century American society.

Summary

America's technological society is evolving at an alarming pace. The personnel requirements of the twenty-first–century workforce are vastly different than those of twenty-five years ago. Unfortunately, our schools have not kept pace with this economic revolution. Our educational system is producing the same type of "future workers" as it did a quarter of a century ago. Much of the teaching methodologies remain the same, as have much of the students' learned work behaviors. In order for America to keep pace with the increasingly global economy, we need to start examining what today's businesses require from our graduates, and make the necessary adjustments in our educational program.

The age of the solitary worker completing one particular task is quickly fading. Today's businesses are searching for individuals who are comfortable with operating in work groups on long-term projects. They are being more selective in matching personnel to the tasks required in order to maintain a workforce who can reach their potential, using the most modern technology in order to efficiently and effectively solve problems.

No longer are businesses worried about hiring graduates with specific prerequisite knowledge. Information is evolving too rapidly. The specialized computer program taught in high school is obsolete by the time the graduate reaches the workforce. As a result, businesses regularly educate new employees in the material required for that particular job. However, what they cannot do is teach these new workers how to successfully function in this new environment. For this, they look to America's educational system to prepare the next generation for these new requirements of the business community.

This is the goal of the cooperative work group concept. Through the incorporation of cooperative learning (group investigation), brain research (the multiple intelligences), and the active integration of the most modern technology into the curriculum (the Internet), we can produce students who can succeed in any situation or environment in the twenty-first–century workplace.

Part IV

Some Practical Examples of Teacher Unit Plans

The following unit plans were written by current classroom teachers. Each plan is a self-contained unit, and incorporates the three cooperative work group concept areas: the use of advanced cooperative learning, incorporation of the multiple intelligences, and integration of Internet resources. These plans are to serve as practical examples of the types of teaching described throughout this book. Teachers can either

• Use these lessons as is, with minor modifications to fit available materials and specific student academic levels

• Adapt them to fit their own particular classrooms, making significant modifications to make them applicable to their curricula

• Study them as models for creating their own units, paying particular attention to the structure and components of the units and incorporating the methodology for their own original curricular units

Each of the unit plans attempt to be general in nature so as to be applicable to the greatest number of teachers. The curricular material and methodologies can easily be adapted to any level within the displayed grade span, and to most classroom situations, including those with ELL or special education students.

As demonstrated in these sample units, there is considerable integration of different subject areas within most cooperative work group experiences. For example, curricular background information is usually found in the Social Studies realm—even if the experience is primarily one in the areas of the Language Arts, Science, or Math. The Arts can be integrated into virtually any unit, especially if the teacher plans for the integration of all of the multiple intelligences. When constructing cooperative work group units, the teacher needs to look at the curricular material in a broad sense. The teacher-created experiences included demonstrate this concept.

This section includes the following four general curricular units:

Primary Subject Area(s)	Title of Unit	General Grade Range
Science	A Trip to the Rainforest	3–8
Language Arts/History	The World of *Zlata's Diary*	5–12
History/The Arts	Ancient Egypt—The Afterlife	4–10
Math	Real Life with Fractions, Decimals, Ratios, Proportions, and Percentages	5–9

For ease of teacher use, each unit follows a similar format. The format is designed to cover the basic components of the cooperative work group experience, and may *not* be inclusive of all of the planning areas required of an onsite administrator or university instructor. In those situations, the plans should be altered so as to better meet one's personal requirements.

Each of the units include the following areas:

- Objectives
- Materials
- Internet Sites to Use Throughout the Unit
- Method
- Assessment Suggestions
- Use of the Multiple Intelligences
- Special Teacher Notes

The following is a more detailed description of what each of these areas encompasses:

Objectives

The first area presented is some basic behavioral objectives that all students should meet, regardless of age or the teacher adaptations. These few goals are core to the overall unit. As the unit is modified for specific classroom use, additional behavioral objectives should be added.

Materials

Next is a list of basic materials that are necessary for the activities listed throughout the unit. If the teacher picks and chooses among the activities, then this material list also needs to be altered. Curricular listings, such as "books" and "videos," are purposely stated in general terms whenever possible to allow for variations in a teacher's library resource center, and within the academic levels of the students.

Internet Sites to Use Throughout the Unit

This section includes all of the Internet sites that are mentioned in the "Method" section. Included are the title of the site, the URL, and a brief description of the material to be located. It is important to note that these sites are personal favorites of the unit authors. Many of them are teacher- or student-created Web sites, especially those created through the "Webquest" educational technology program. Therefore, the sites may not be in existence by the time the reader attempts the unit. When this occurs, use the steps outlined in Part III for locating new educational Internet sites, sites that would provide the required curricular material for that teaching situation.

Method

A simple, step-by-step methodology is included with a sequential outline of the various activities for the entire unit. Included is a description of the "problem," roles, and tasks of the cooperative work groups. All of the information in this section is presented in as general terms as possible. Therefore, when teaching this unit, the methodology needs to be adapted to the specific academic level of the students using the material.

Assessment Suggestions

Since these lessons cover a wide range of ages, this section provides a couple of very basic suggestions for assessment of student progress at the end of the unit. Assessment must be tailored to the individual goals of the teacher and the academic level of the students. Please refer back to the assessment section in Part I for more direction on how best to assess the cooperative work group experience.

Use of the Multiple Intelligences

A simple multiple intelligences chart is provided to demonstrate how each of the intelligences is addressed at some point during the unit. The list is not exhaustive, but rather serves as a teacher check to ensure that each of the categories is integrated into the unit at some point.

Special Teacher Notes

This section is provided for the author of the unit to add any specific suggestions or comments to make the unit more meaningful and helpful to the reader.

Teachers often find themselves with specific types of lesson/unit plan formats that they are required to write, be it in a school or a university classroom setting. The material in these cooperative work group units is rather basic and can be adapted and manipulated to fit any specific plan format required of the reader. *The goal of this section is to demonstrate how a cooperative work group unit can be organized.* As stated throughout this book, the important idea to remember is that the teacher can adapt the material in a fashion that leads to success for that particular teacher. The "structure" is not critical. The curricular material and its presentation are what is important. However, for the benefit of those who want to use the "lesson plan" format promoted in this section, a sample, blank form is included in Resource D.

Subject Area: Science

A Trip to the Rainforest

GRADE RANGE: 3–8

Objectives

At the end of this unit the students will:

- Understand the various flora, fauna, and native inhabitants of the rainforest

- Analyze the problems facing those affected by the destruction of the rainforest, both locally and globally

- Synthesize the material on the rainforest into both a "rainforest experience" and a "creative brochure" project

- Evaluate the current state of the rainforest in today's society

Materials

- Books, videos, and activity packets concerning characteristics of life in the rainforest. (These are available from any educational supply store, educational publisher, and on the Internet).

- Tapes of sounds of the rainforest (found in any nature-oriented store)

- For the Rainstick Project:
    - Paper towel rolls
    - Toothpicks (rounded ends)
    - Pins
    - Glue
    - Needle-nose pliers
    - Masking tape

- Thick paper (similar to tag board)
- Dry beans and rice mix
- Brown construction paper
- Clear tape
- Markers
- Thin yarn

Internet Sites to Use Throughout the Unit

Rainforest Action Network. www.ran.org/ran. This site explains what people and organizations are currently doing to protect the rainforest. The material includes fact sheets that define characteristics of the rainforest on the students' levels. The site also supplies activity sheets and basic information about the people and animals of the ecosystem.

Science in the Rainforest: Take a Walk in the Rainforest. www.pbs.org/tal/costa_rica/rainwalk.html. On this site, individuals take themselves on a walk in the rainforest. The teacher and students can choose what they want to investigate, selecting from topics such as monkeys, plants, nightlife, habitats, and birds. The site provides numerous photographs and detailed information presented on the students' level.

Method

(Material for these activities is derived from various education sources accumulated prior to the teaching of the unit.)

1. Create a bulletin board on the rainforest, using many of the pictures/activity book materials from the sources above. Include a KWL chart (What We Know, What We Want to Know, What We Learned), which is filled out throughout the unit.

2. Provide an overview of the rainforest to the students—geography, introduction to animal and plant life, and finally an overview of what the students will learn.

3. Discuss and provide examples of the four distinct layers of the rainforest:
    - The forest floor
    - The understory
    - The canopy
    - The emergent layer

4. Discuss and provide examples of the various animals residing in the rainforest:
    - Their types
    - The layers in which they live
    - Their eating habits and daily routines.

5. Discuss and provide examples of the various plants of the rainforest:
    - Their types
    - The layers in which they are found
    - Their position in the global ecosystem
    - Their use as medicine for humans (discovered and undiscovered)

6. Discuss and provide examples of the multitude of products that derive from the rainforest.

117

7. Discuss and provide examples of the people who make their homes in the rainforest:
   - Their lives
   - Daily routines
   - History
   - Economy

8. Discuss the current destruction of the rainforest, including the roles and motivations of the following:
   - Outside corporations
   - Local governments
   - The indigenous people of the area

9. Discuss current conservation projects that are being conducted in America, in their community, and in the region of the rainforest.

10. Create rainsticks:
    - On the paper towel rolls, mark dots on the diagonal line (where the paper comes together) every 1/2 inch.

    - Take a pin and poke a hole through each dot. (It is important not to use other objects that would create a hole that is too big).

    - Stick a toothpick through a hole. Go straight across and poke through the other side, using the pin to open a second hole. Do this all the way down the tube through every dot. (When looking inside the tube, the toothpicks should be "crisscrossing" all the way down).

    - Put glue around every toothpick where it goes into the paper roll, all the way down the sides.

    - After the glue dries, take the needle nose pliers and snip off the outside pieces of the toothpicks, as close to the paper towel roll as possible.

    - Completely wrap the tube with masking tape, leaving the two ends open.

    - Cutting a circle slightly larger than the end of the paper roll, cover one end and seal with masking tape.

    - Pour in 1/2–3/4 cup of the bean/rice mixture. In determining the amount, listen to the sound it makes as it flows through the tube. There should be just enough to trickle down slowly, sounding like a real rainstick.

    - Cover up the other end with a circular piece of paper as you did with the other side, sealing the roll.

    - Cover the rainstick with brown construction paper, securing with clear tape.

    - Take the markers and create a design on the rainstick. Use the yarn for macramé. Be creative!

11. Students are placed in cooperative work groups to "create" a rain forest in the classroom.
    - The composition of the groups should primarily be determined by the amount and level of the reading required for the tasks selected.

- The curricular material for the groups is derived from the books, Internet resources, and the previous classroom activities and discussions throughout the unit.

- Group problem: How can they recreate a rainforest experience within their classroom to share with other students and their parents?

- Groups include the following:

    - *Vegetation Group.* Their role is to create vines, plants, and other vegetation to hang and display around the room
    - *Animal Group.* Their role is to develop animals for the rainforest, using pictures and three-dimensional activity book materials
    - *Native People Group.* Their role is to dress up and recreate some aspect of daily life in the rainforest, either cultural or food related
    - *Tour Guide Group.* Their role is to create a "tour" through the rainforest, using actual facts from the real rainforest.

12. As a final project, students are put in cooperative work groups to work on a "travel brochure" for a trip to the rainforest. They use the educational materials that are discovered throughout the unit.

- The composition of the groups should be mixed equally since the tasks for the groups are identical.

- The curricular material for the groups is derived from the books, Internet resources, and the previous classroom activities and discussions throughout the unit.

- Group problem: The students are the owners of a travel company "selling" a trip to the rainforest. Using the information discovered in the unit, they design an original "Travel Brochure" that is meant to excite someone enough to "hire" them for their trip. The brochure must contain the following sections:
    - A cover design
    - Lodging and food
    - Types of animals to see
    - Types of plants to see
    - A map, including topography
    - Advertisements

Assessment Suggestions

- Create a rubric for the final project (the travel brochure) that is determined by the amount of information and effort the students incorporate into their project. The students' grade level and abilities will determine the levels of the rubric. An adjusted group grade can be given to groups where there is a discrepancy in the amount of work done by the individuals.

- If there is specific curricular material to be covered in this unit, an objective test can be used, fashioned to both the students' levels and the material covered in the experience. A good portion of the test should be open-ended, so as to allow for variations in each student's experience.

Use of the Multiple Intelligences

Intelligence	How it is addressed in the unit
Verbal-linguistic	The written material on the rainforest; the travel brochure
Logical-mathematical	Investigation of the systematic causes of the destruction of the rainforests
Visual-spatial	The pictures of the rainforest; the rainstick activity; the travel brochure
Bodily-kinesthetic	Acting out the various facets of life in the rainforest during the simulated rainforest activity
Musical	Listening to music and sounds of the rainforest
Interpersonal	The cooperative work group activities
Intrapersonal	Personal choices made during the rainstick activity and work within the cooperative work groups
Naturalist	The study of the flora and fauna of the rainforest ecosystem

Special Teacher Notes

There are only two Internet sites noted, as they are both extremely comprehensive and should provide all of the information that you would probably require. The two sites also contain links to additional information. If you want other choices for online material, search for "rainforest" in METACRAWLER or another search engine.

—Submitted by Melodie Bitter
Los Angeles, California

Subject Area: Language Arts/History

The World of Zlata's Diary

GRADE RANGE: 5–12

Objectives

At the end of this unit the students will:

- Understand the current political situation in Bosnia

- Analyze the living conditions in Bosnia through the use of *Zlata's Diary* along with current Internet resources

- Synthesize the material learned into a final project/presentation on the conditions and situations facing the people in that region and the implications for the rest of the world

- Evaluate the causes of the conflict in Bosnia and how they could affect the other potential religious and ethnic situations in Europe and around the world

Materials

- The book *Zlata's Diary,* by Zlata Filipovic
- Maps of the region
- Writing materials
- Large paper for creating maps

- Examples of American protest songs of the 1960s, and those coming out of Bosnia and Eastern Europe since the Communist decline

Internet Sites to Use Throughout the Unit

How Big Is Bosnia-Herzegovina? www.kakarigi.net/homeland/maps/bih_big.htm. The site consists of a map of Bosnia-Herzegovina, comparing it with the state of Florida.

Map Collections. web.nps.navy.mil/~library/mapcollection.htm. The site includes Bosnia Map Sites, Dudley Knox Library Maps of Croatia and Bosnia-Herzegovina, Bosnia maps from Perry-Castaneda Library Map Collection, Bosnia Link Maps, and Maps from Caltech. (This site also provides links to the listed maps and many more.)

ABCNEWS.com: A Beginners Guide to the Balkans. abcnews.go.com/sections/world/balkans_content. This is a great general site for basic information on the conflict. The material is presented on a student, versus an adult, news-oriented level.

BBC News: KOSOVO. news.bbc.co.uk/hi/english/special_report/1998/kosovo. This site is more advanced and "news oriented" than the ABC news site.

Merriam-Webster's Geographical Dictionary, Third Edition. www.m-w.com/geog-promo/bosnia.htm. A brief history of the area is included on this site.

Embassy of Bosnia and Herzegovina, Washington, D.C. www.bosnianembassy.org. This site provides "official" history, information on current affairs, and contacts for Bosnia.

Bosnia HomePage at Caltech. www.cco.caltech.edu/~bosnia/bosnia.html. This site will connect you with the top sites on the Internet. Approximately seven pages of links are provided.

Say Hello in the Serbo-Croatian Language. www.ipl.org/youth/hello/serbocroat.html. The students can learn simple examples of the language of the land on this site.

Bosnian Music. www.tamburaweb.com/bosnia.htm. This site includes excellent reference material on Bosnian music.

Method

1. The class reads and discusses the book, *Zlata's Diary.* In order to create empathy with Zlata, a concentration should be made on her feelings and personal experiences throughout the ordeal.

2. The students are placed into cooperative work groups. The group problem: They are members of an International Committee to Investigate the Problems in Bosnia.

- The groups each take on one of the following "identities": the different factions in the conflict, a neighboring country with similar problems, American foreign policy advisors, and any other areas that you feel would be appropriate for the age and ability levels of your students.

- Group composition should directly address the reading and academic levels required of the online material.

- The students investigate the problem, based on material discovered through the Internet sites that are provided. If online access is limited, much of the information can be downloaded by the teacher and placed in vertical files.

- As a final activity, the groups present their findings to the class as a whole, as part of a "symposium" on the Bosnian problem. Each group should remember to present information from the particular viewpoint of their "identity."

3. At any point, throughout the unit, the students can complete the following activities either as a whole class, through individual work, and/or within the groups:

- Using a Venn diagram compare/contrast the wartime lives of Anne Frank and Zlata Filipovic. Determine if it can be said that Zlata is a modern-day Anne Frank.

- Create any or all of the following maps:
  a. Create two maps of the Balkans—one before the countries sought independence and the second, a current map of the area. Locate some of the landmarks mentioned in the book, *Zlata's Diary.*
  b. Using the same scale for a map of your state and a map of the Balkans, create one map of the Balkans with an overlay of your state. This will help the students understand the size of the Balkans.
  c. Create an outline map of the Balkans or trace one for completing the map tasks. Feel free to delete or add sites from the lists. Locate the following places identified in *Zlata's Diary* and label the countries and land forms. Indicate by color the countries that once were a part of Yugoslavia:
     - Sarajevo
     - Jahorina
     - Crnotina
     - Otes
     - Dubrovnik
     - Adriatic Sea
     - Albania
     - Austria
     - Black Sea
     - Bosnia-Herzegovina
     - Bulgaria
     - Croatia
     - Greece
     - Hungary
     - Italy
     - Macedonia
     - Montenegro
     - Romania
     - Serbia
     - Slovenia

- Write an imaginary conversation between Anne Frank and Zlata Filipovic discussing their wartime lives and perform it as a skit. If needed, other family members could be included, such as parents, so everyone in the group can participate.

- Compare the civil rights/war protests songs of the 1960s to the songs coming from Balkans since the decline of Communism.

- Describe and discuss the temporary/permanent changes to the environment due to the war in the Balkans.

4. As a final activity, discuss the history of the conflict, concentrating on the rights denied people in Bosnia. Compare that loss of their rights to the rights guaranteed in our Constitution, specifically in the Bill of Rights. Create a Venn Diagram comparing and contrasting rights allowed and denied in the United States and Bosnia.

Assessment Suggestions

- Create a rubric for the final project (the symposium on Bosnia) that is determined by the amount of information and effort the students incorporate into their presentation. The students' grade level and abilities will determine the levels of the rubric. An adjusted group grade can be given to groups where there is a discrepancy in the amount of work by the individuals.

- Material discovered through the cooperative work group investigations can be incorporated into a test on the students' comprehension of the book, *Zlata's Diary*. Take care that if there is specific information that the students need to discover for the assessment that they are provided with the URLs, the material, or, at a minimum, a list of the material they will be asked about.

Use of the Multiple Intelligences

Intelligence	How it is addressed in the unit
Verbal-linguistic	Reading the book *Zlata's Diary*; the research for the cooperative work group project
Logical-mathematical	Creation of the various Venn Diagrams
Visual-spatial	The map projects
Bodily/Kinesthetic	The Anne Frank/Zlata conversation/skit
Musical	Listening to the songs of the 60s and from Eastern Europe today
Interpersonal	The work in the cooperative work groups
Intrapersonal	Individual choice, made in the cooperative work group research, and the personal writings created throughout the unit
Naturalist	The discussion of the environment of Bosnia

Additional Teacher Notes

- I have worked with the at risk for many years and found that the normal way of selecting cooperative groups would not work in group selection. Instead, I formed my own way of grouping and have used it since that time.
  - Students are to record two lists. On the first list, they are to list three people with whom they can work well (not necessarily best friends, but a good working relationship). The second list can be only one person. If a student believes there is someone in the class that they absolutely cannot work with, then they may record ONE name only. The papers are then folded for privacy and students either drop their lists in my basket as they leave class, or they pass the lists forward. Then I start grouping. I honor everyone's "cannot work with" list. This really isn't as hard as it may seem as many leave the second list blank or often write they are willing to work with anyone.
  - Next, I go through the "good working relationship" list and try to honor at least one person from that list in grouping. All the time I also try to keep a student leader and one with a high spatial, bodily-kinesthetic, and musical multiple intelligence in each group if possible. Groups vary from four to five in size according to the number of students in the class.

—Submitted by Ginny Hoover
Garden City, Kansas

Ancient Egypt— The Afterlife

GRADE RANGE: 4–10

Objectives

At the end of this unit the students will:

- Understand the various features, religious beliefs, and customs of the Ancient Egyptian burial practices.

- Synthesize the various features, religious beliefs, and customs of the Ancient Egyptian burial practices into an original project where they create and develop a "tomb" for a Pharaoh.

- Evaluate which customs and features of Egyptian life would be most appropriate to include for their "tomb."

Materials

- Books and videos on ancient Egypt, primarily dealing with their customs concerning the afterlife
- Glue
- Poster board
- Markers
- Scissors
- Construction paper
- Newspaper
- Papier-mâché
- Chicken wire (for papier-mâché)
- Paint
- Paint brushes
- Drop cloths

- Butcher paper
- Rulers
- 2 empty refrigerator boxes

Internet Sites to Use Throughout the Unit

Egypt Pyramids Pharaohs Hieroglyphs: Mark Millmore's Ancient Egypt. www.eyelid. co.uk. This Web site gives detailed information on kings and queens, the burial process, and Egyptian writing. Plus, the Web site also allows the students to send cards, order books and screensavers, and play games.

The Ancient Egypt Site. www.geocities.com/amenhotep.geo. Explore the history of Ancient Egypt, Saqqara (City of the Dead), and the Egyptian language at this site. There are also several resources and resource links included.

Ancient Egypt: A Webquest. www.plainfield.k12.in.us/hschool/webq/webq33/ aegypt.htm. This is an interactive site for children where they can tour Ancient Egypt by following a series of steps. The end product is a journal that includes several items (supply list, illustrations of the mummification process, a timeline, and more).

Welcome to Akhet Egyptology. www.akhet.co.uk. At this site the students can find out who the Ancient Egyptians worshiped, what temples and statues they left behind, and the Pharaohs they followed. They can also learn about mummies and what is kept in their tombs.

Mummification. www.tir.com/~lanata/mummification.html. This site details every step of mummification.

Egindex. www.snaithprimary.eril.net/egindex.htm. This is an interactive Web site that talks about the Egyptian language, paintings, artifacts, temples, and landscapes.

NOVA Online/Pyramids/Hot Science: Scaling the Pyramids. www.pbs.org/wgbh/nova/ pyramid/geometry. This Web site details Egyptian information including pyramids and the Sphinx, displaying them to scale.

Neferchichi's Tomb: KIDS PAGE. www.neferchichi.com/kids.html. At this site, the students explore Ancient Egypt and learn about mummies, hieroglyphics, gods, and pharaohs.

The Food Timeline. www.gti.net/mocolib1/kid/food.html. This is a site that puts the introduction of various foods on a timeline, and gives a detailed history of how that particular food was used through time.

Method

1. The students are placed in heterogeneous cooperative work groups, since the tasks of each group are identical. Group problem: They are members of the royal court of Pharaoh Maydupkingha. The Pharaoh has just died, and the students have to plan out all burial procedures using the customs and rituals of ancient Egyptians. The following procedures can be conducted partially as a whole class, or within the

individual groups depending on the number of computers available. If there is adequate accessibility, all of the research can be undertaken by the groups. If there is limited accessibility, much of the online material can be printed and placed into vertical files for the groups to manipulate and use.

2. Have the groups to go to MUMMIFICATION to learn the basics about mummies, why they were created, and the steps that it takes to create a mummy. Once the groups have finished looking at those sites, they should go to WELCOME TO AKHET EGYPTOLOGY and click on the "clickable mummy" tab. Once the page downloads, there is a mummy on the left side of the Web site. That is the "clickable mummy." Click on areas of the mummy and learn how each part of the body is preserved. Once the groups have discovered the mummification process, the class should come together and discuss what they learned during an initial debriefing session.

3. The groups should use the Web site list provided to find pictures that represent Egypt (for example, pyramids, sphinx, Pharaohs, gods and goddesses, Nile River, Hieroglyphics [can be used as the heading], mummies, masks). The groups should be encouraged to find a statement within the Web site, or write their own statement, describing the picture and its significance to Egypt (location, description of the item, what makes the item important to Egyptians). Once the groups have all of the pictures they want to use, have them create a paper-cut mural using the pictures they have found. Under each picture the students should write or paste a typed copy of the description they found or came up with.

4. The students should be encouraged to go to EGYPT PYRAMIDS PHARAOHS HIEROGLYPHS—MARK MILLMORE'S ANCIENT EGYPT along with THE ANCIENT EGYPT SITE and learn about the pyramids and tombs in Egypt. Once the students are finished touring the Web site, they construct a 3D map and a 3D pyramid from the list of pyramids listed in the Web site. This will be the resting place for their Pharaoh. After the 3D map and pyramid are completed, the students should finish the project by typing or writing a brief historical explanation of the pyramid.

5. The students then view some Web sites from the list provided and learn about different Egyptian tombs. Once the students are done viewing the Web sites, they choose one of the tombs and create a poster about the tomb their Pharaoh will occupy in his pyramid.

6. The students visit ANCIENT EGYPT: A WEBQUEST. At the beginning of the Web site, there is a list of tasks that the students have to complete. Some of the subject areas include

- Creating a supply list needed for their trip
- Exploring and examining a list of three sites in Egypt
- Working with a timeline of the pharaohs and queens
- Studying a list of functions about each part of pyramids

Once the students have read through the tasks, there are step-by-step instructions to follow to complete each of them. Within each of the instructions there are links to uncover the information necessary to complete the activities. Once the tasks are complete, the groups create a poster of their writings and any interesting information or facts discovered in the Web site.

7. The groups need to research hieroglyphics from the list of Web sites provided. They then write a hieroglyphic message about their Pharaoh that would be displayed inside their tomb. The groups can draw or trace the hieroglyphics.

8. The groups now create a coffin and treasures to be included inside. They need to draw Egyptian symbols on the tomb (gods, goddesses, and hieroglyphics) and make a mask on the lid. The treasures should include things such as dried-up food, and household objects.

9. The groups should review information about pyramids from the website NOVA ONLINE/PYRAMIDS/HOT SCIENCE: SCALING THE PYRAMIDS. They then write a story to someone back home as if they were building a pyramid. The letter should include the following information:
   - What are they going through?
   - Where are they living?
   - What is the temperature like?
   - How long are their workdays?
   - How long is it taking to build?
   - How many people are helping them?

10. Invite the students to view EGINDEX and learn about Egyptian art. Once the students have finished viewing the site, they should paint on the "walls" of their Pharaoh's tomb like the Egyptians. This can be completed as a class by using two walls of the classroom covered with brown paper. The students should base their drawings on the pictures they saw in the Web site (Egyptian statues, hieroglyphics, pyramids, gods, goddesses).

11. After reading in books and searching on the Internet about the mummification process and the steps in the burial process, the students should create a "book of the dead." The book of the dead is a document that the Egyptians wrote about the life of the individual.

12. On the day that the cooperative work group projects are due, have an entire "class event." (These activities and events should be adapted to the age and sophistication level of the students). Before the students come to class, have two refrigerator boxes prepared in the doorway of the classroom so students have to crawl through the passageway to get into the classroom. The classroom should be decorated like a tomb. Use the materials that the groups created to decorate the room. Encourage them to come dressed as Egyptians for the next day of class. Using the web site THE FOOD TIMELINE, investigate different foods that may have been eaten at this time, having the class prepare some examples before the party. Stations can also be set up with Egyptian games for the groups to complete during the day's activities. As the students come into the classroom, there should be nametags with their names written in hieroglyphics.

13. As a follow-up, have the class investigate mummification further. There are several places around the world where mummies can be found, not just in Egypt. Have students refer to NEFERCHICHI'S TOMB: KIDS PAGE and learn about the different locations of mummies around the world.

14. Other activities that can be included within the unit:

- After learning about the burial process for Egyptians from the Internet and books, divide the class into groups of four or five and encourage them to write a story as if they were on a journey to Egypt to locate an old Egyptian tomb.

- Within the story the groups should answer the following questions:
  - Where in Egypt did you go (city)?
  - What did you find?
  - What did it look like?
  - Was the mummy there?
  - Could you tell if thieves had gotten to the tomb before you, or did they come while you were there?
  - What is on the walls?
  - Is there any writing?
  - Can you decode it?

- After reading in books and searching on the Internet about the Sphinx, have the students make a papier-mâché Sphinx out of wire and papier-mâché. The Sphinx will be of a much smaller size, but should be as realistic looking as possible.

Assessment Suggestions

- Create a rubric for the cooperative work group activity (the Pharaoh's tomb) that is determined by the amount of information and effort they incorporate into their project. The students' grade level and abilities will determine the levels of the rubric. An adjusted group grade can be given to groups where there is a discrepancy in the amount of work by the individuals.

- If there is specific curricular material to be covered in this unit, an objective test can be used, fashioned to both the students' level and the material covered in the experience. A good portion of the test should be open-ended so as to allow for variations in each student's experience. Basic core informational areas that all groups should cover during the project include:
  - What are mummies?
  - How is a mummy made?
  - Why did the Egyptians believe in mummification?
  - Where are mummies buried (building)? Were they always buried in the same structure?
  - Were people the only ones to be mummified?
  - What kinds of objects were placed in the burial chamber with the mummy in the coffin and outside of the mummies coffin?
  - What is an example of a burial chamber for Egyptians?
  - What kind of "decorations" covered the walls of Egyptian burial chambers?
  - What is believed to be the mummies' afterlife?
  - How are pyramids made?
  - How many kinds of pyramids are there?
  - What are the names of the different kinds of pyramids?
  - Who built the pyramids?
  - What happened during a funeral procession in Ancient Egypt?
  - What are hieroglyphics?
  - What is a sphinx?
  - Where are mummies located? (Geographically: Is Egypt the only country?)

Use of the Multiple Intelligences

Intelligence	How it is addressed in the unit
Verbal-linguistic	Reading the material on Egyptian beliefs and burial practices
Logical-mathematical	Studying the steps involved in the mummification process
Visual-spatial	The art projects throughout the unit
Bodily/Kinesthetic	Taking the role of artisans creating a tomb for their Pharaoh and acting out the roles on the final day
Musical	Investigating musical instruments to include within the tomb
Interpersonal	The cooperative work group activity
Intrapersonal	Individual choices made within the groups and individual work throughout the unit
Naturalist	Studying the animals involved in Ancient Egyptian culture and their place within the religious beliefs

Additional Teacher Notes

Be sure to check out all of these Internet sites before you begin your unit. Many of them are teacher and/or student created and may no longer be working, especially those created under the Webquest program. There are many duplicate sites available, however, if you need a replacement. Check out general education web sites along with search engines.

—Submitted by Kelley Tressler
York, Pennsylvania

Real Life With Fractions, Decimals, Ratios, Proportions, and Percentages

GRADE RANGE: 4–9

Objectives

At the end of this unit the students will:

• Understand how fractions, decimals, ratios, proportions, and percentages relate to everyday life

• Analyze the numeric data and calculate it as necessary for the situation

• Synthesize the material learned into a final presentation using the math concepts of fractions, decimals, ratios, proportions, and percentages

• Evaluate data in order to adapt it to a variety of real-life situations

Materials

• A large turkey and the cooking materials necessary

• Food materials for the side dishes and desserts to be determined as the groups decide on their choices

• Poster board and writing materials

Internet Sites to Use Throughout the Unit

History/Social Studies Web Site for K-12 Teachers. execpc.com/~dboals/boals.html. This site has links to all of the information your students will need to conduct research for the Thanksgiving feast. Select "American History Sources" and "Colonial" for hundreds of educational Internet sites. The site can also be used for some of the background material for the community service group by looking for titles in the "Humanities/Art" and the "News/Current Events" links.

Mimi's Cyber-Kitchen. www.cyber-kitchen.com. This Web site is a great site to use to locate recipes of all sorts. Look through the recipe links and the "How to Find Food On the Web" link. Try to find recipes that utilize fractional measurements. Also look for those that feed fewer than eight people (which allows you to automatically have to expand the amounts).

VolunteerMatch. www.volunteermatch.org. Use this site to locate food banks and contact information within your local geographical area. Simply type in your zip code and click "go." Then pull down the menus to select the appropriate mileage radius and to search for "Hunger."

Yahoo! www.yahoo.com. This site can provide local information on supermarkets and community food pantries in your area. Go to "Regional: US States," select your state, city, and then appropriate subheading.

Method

1. The students are placed in heterogeneous cooperative work groups, since the tasks of each group are basically identical. Group problem: They are conducting a Thanksgiving feast for the class and their parents. Every task that is required will be looked at as a form of math problem, using fractions, decimals, ratios, proportions, and/or percentages. Also included with this project will be a community service project.

2. The teacher can acquire a "free" turkey from one of the supermarkets, or one can be bought and/or donated to the class. Individual students can each make side dishes and desserts, based on the data that those groups produce.

3. The following are the groups and their tasks:

- *Turkey Group.* Math issues for the group:
  - Look through the newspaper the week before Thanksgiving and mathematically determine which local market has the best buy on a turkey. Use ratio, proportion, and percentage to determine the answer.
  - Using ratio, determine how the weight of the turkey and cooking time are related.
  - Many people love the turkey skin. How much skin is on the bird? Figure out the approximate surface area, using fractions, decimals, and percentages.

- *Side Dish Group.* Math issues for the group:
  - Using MIMI'S CYBER-KITCHEN web site, look for various recipes for the students to use for the feast. Using ratios, proportion, and knowledge of fractions, adapt all recipes to feed twelve people.

  – Using local supermarkets that have online information, determine the best buy for the various ingredients. Use ratios and proportions for the calculations.

- *Dessert Group.* Math issues for the group:
  – As with the side dishes group, they use MIMI'S CYBER-KITCHEN Web site, look for various recipes for the students to use for the feast. Using ratios, proportions, and knowledge of fractions, adapt all recipes to feed twelve people.
  – Determine size of pie pieces based on the number of participants and the number of pies available. Using decimals and percentages, determine how much pie each participant can have.
  – Create "math problems," such as—after determining the surface area of the pies, how much whipped cream will they need for a 1/2-inch layer on each pie?

- *Community Service Group.* Using the Internet and/or the phone book, contact food pantries for the poor in the area. Math issues for the group:
  – Investigate how much food they recommend to feed a family of four for a month. Then determine how much food each participant should bring to the feast as a donation for a food pantry.

- *Historical Group.* Using the HISTORY/SOCIAL STUDIES WEB SITE FOR K-12 TEACHERS, this group investigates the pilgrims, and presents a report to the class at the feast. Math issues for the group:
  – Determine the percentages and ratios of a number of different variables: for example, men, women, children in the group; how many survived the first year.

4. Throughout the unit, each of the groups keeps records of their computations and data, and creates poster-size charts of their calculations. They present their findings to the class, demonstrating to the class how fractions, decimals, ratios, proportions, and percentages are used in everyday life—that is, in their Thanksgiving feast.

Assessment Suggestions

- Create a rubric based on the amount of work and effort for each group member

- Have each group create a few sample problems, based on their presentation, for a whole class test on fractions, decimals, ratios, proportions, and percentages

Use of the Multiple Intelligences

Intelligence	How it is addressed in the unit
Verbal-linguistic	The written material on the Internet
Logical-mathematical	The various mathematical problems
Visual-spatial	The poster board presentations
Bodily/Kinesthetic	The making of the food

Musical	Nothing naturally fits in this area, so the teacher plays quiet music throughout some of the work sessions. If possible, locate some music from the Pilgrims' time period and play that at some point in the unit.
Interpersonal	The work in the cooperative work groups
Intrapersonal	Individual choice, made in the cooperative work group research
Naturalist	The discussion of the environment of Plymouth and how it affected the pilgrims and their diet

—Submitted by Rob Schuck
Los Angeles, California

Resource A

Index of URLs

Bibliography of North American Indians

nmnhwww.si.edu/anthro/outreach/Indbibl/bibliogr.html

Children's Literature Web Guide

www.ucalgary.ca/~dkbrown/index.html

Desert Life in the American Southwest

www.desertusa.com/life.html

54 Ways You Can Help the Homeless

www.earthsystems.org/ways

The Food Timeline

www.gti.net/mocolib1/kid/food.html

Free Ocean Life Pictures!

www.1stopwallpaper.com/webshots.html

Frontier Culture Museum

frontier.vipnet.org

Historical Text Archive

historicaltextarchive.com

History/Social Studies Web Site for K-12 Teachers

execpc.com/~dboals/boals.html

The Hunger Site

www.thehungersite.com/cgi-bin/WebObjects/CTDSites

Kathy Schrock's Guide for Educators

school.discovery.com/schrockguide

Kids Corner International Year of the Ocean

www.yoto98.noaa.gov/links.htm

Lycos

www.lycos.com

Math Forum

forum.swarthmore.edu

Metacrawler

www.metacrawler.com

Mongolian and Tuvinian Music

userpage.fu-berlin.de/~corff/im/Musik/overview.Music.html

The Northern Great Plains: 1880–1920

memory.loc.gov/ammem/award97/ndfahtml

Ocean Collection for Kids

www.calstatela.edu/faculty/eviau/edit557/oceans

The Old-Timers Page

waltonfeed.com/old

Science Education Zone

tlc.ousd.k12.ca.us/~acody

Teachers Helping Teachers

www.pacificnet.net/~mandel

Volunteer Match

www.volunteermatch.org

Welcome to Life in the Ocean

www.calstatela.edu/faculty/eviau/edit557/oceans/norma/onfrm.htm

World Wide Arts Resource

wwar.com

Yahoo!

www.yahoo.com

Resource B

Student Multiple Intelligence Assessments

The following student Multiple Intelligence assessments have been reprinted with permission. They include:

Two separate student assessments created by the staff of the Teachers' Curriculum Institute in Palo Alto, California ("Identifying Your Multiple Intelligences: Assessment 1 & 2"). These are assessments that are used by the students. Assessment 1 is more appropriate for students in Grades 3–8. Assessment 2 works best with students in Grades 6–12.

The second assessment, created by Thomas Armstrong (2000), is to be completed by the teacher, based on personal knowledge and observations of the student.

Please note that the two assessments from *History Alive!* do not include questions that pertain to the 8th Multiple Intelligence, the Naturalist Intelligence. Assessments including this Intelligence had not been created at the time of publication, but are expected in the next edition of the *History Alive!* materials.

Identifying Your Multiple Intelligences: Assessment 1

This quiz will help you identify your areas of strongest intelligence. Read each statement. If it expresses some characteristic of yours and sounds true for the most part, jot down "T." If it doesn't, mark "F." If the statement is sometimes true and sometimes false, leave it blank.

1. _____ I'd rather draw a map than give someone verbal directions.
2. _____ If I am angry or happy, I usually know why.
3. _____ I can play (or used to play) a musical instrument.
4. _____ I compose songs or raps and perform them.
5. _____ I can add or multiply quickly in my head.
6. _____ I help friends deal with feelings because I deal with my own feelings well.
7. _____ I like to work with calculators and computers.
8. _____ I pick up new dance steps quickly.
9. _____ It's easy for me to say what I think in an argument or debate.
10. _____ I enjoy a good lecture, speech, or sermon.
11. _____ I always know north from south no matter where I am.
12. _____ I like to gather together groups of people for parties or special events.
13. _____ I listen to music on the radio, CDs, or cassettes for much of the day.
14. _____ I always understand the drawings that come with new gadgets or appliances.
15. _____ I like to work puzzles and play games.
16. _____ Learning to ride a bike (or to skate) was easy.
17. _____ I am irritated when I hear an argument or statement that sounds illogical.
18. _____ I can convince other people to follow my plans.
19. _____ My sense of balance and coordination is good.
20. _____ I often see patterns and relationships between numbers faster than others.
21. _____ I enjoy building models (or sculpting).
22. _____ I like word games and puns.
23. _____ I can look at an object one way and see it turned backward just as easily.
24. _____ I can identify when there is a key change in a song.
25. _____ I like to work with numbers and figures.
26. _____ I like to sit quietly and reflect on my feelings.
27. _____ Just looking at shapes of buildings and structures is pleasurable to me.
28. _____ I like to hum, whistle, and sing in the shower or when I'm alone.
29. _____ I'm good at athletics.
30. _____ I enjoy writing detailed letters to friends.
31. _____ I'm usually aware of the expression on my face.
32. _____ I'm sensitive to the expressions on other people's faces.
33. _____ I stay in touch with my moods. I have no trouble identifying them.
34. _____ I am sensitive to the moods of others.
35. _____ I have a good sense of what others think of me.

SOURCE: Reprinted with permission from *History Alive!* 1999. Palo Alto, CA: Teachers' Curriculum Institute.

Scoring Your Multiple Intelligences: Assessment 1

Put a "X" in the box for each item you marked with a "T." Add up the number of "Xs." A total of four "Xs" in any category indicates strong ability.

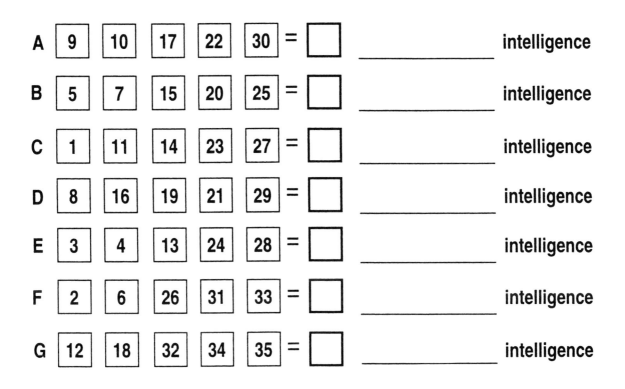

A 9 10 17 22 30 = ☐ _____ intelligence

B 5 7 15 20 25 = ☐ _____ intelligence

C 1 11 14 23 27 = ☐ _____ intelligence

D 8 16 19 21 29 = ☐ _____ intelligence

E 3 4 13 24 28 = ☐ _____ intelligence

F 2 6 26 31 33 = ☐ _____ intelligence

G 12 18 32 34 35 = ☐ _____ intelligence

Teacher Answer Key

Note: Do not reveal these to students until after they have scored their tests.

A = verbal-linguistic
B = logical-mathematical
C = visual-spatial
D = bodily-kinesthetic
E = musical-rhythmic
F = intrapersonal
G = interpersonal

SOURCE: Reprinted with permission from *History Alive!* 1999. Palo Alto, CA: Teachers' Curriculum Institute.

Identifying Your Multiple Intelligences: Assessment 2

For each scenario, rank the 7 options by putting a 1 next to the option you like the most, a 2 by your next choice, and so forth.

1. Planning a Summer Trip

As you plan a summer trip with your friends, you are asked to be responsible for one of the following:
A. ___ Calling all your friends to tell them of the group's plans.
B. ___ Running the errands needed to prepare for the trip.
C. ___ Keeping a trip diary recording your thoughts and feelings.
D. ___ Figuring out the distance to your destination.
E. ___ Preparing songs to sing on the trip.
F. ___ Writing a story about your trip for the newspaper.
G. ___ Mapping the group's journey.

2. What Would Your Friends Say About You?

What would your friends say is true about you?
A. ___ You are happiest when you are talking to other people.
B ___ You like to dance or play sports.
C. ___ You are in touch with your thoughts and feelings.
D. ___ You have fun working on computers or with numbers.
E. ___ You like to sing, rap, or tap out rhythms.
F. ___ You enjoy writing notes or letters.
G. ___ You draw, sketch, or paint well.

3. Pick Your Favorite Electives

Which of the following electives would you most prefer?
A. ___ Peer Counseling
B. ___ Drama
C. ___ Psychology or Comparative Religions
D. ___ Architectural Design, Auto Shop, or Computer Literacy
E. ___ Band or Chorus
F. ___ Creative Writing or Journalism
G. ___ Art

4. Pick Your Favorite Extracurricular Activities

Rank your preferences for the following extracurricular activities:
A. ___ Working as a tutor or joining a team.
B. ___ Taking part in the school play, a dance production, or a martial arts class.
C. ___ Dealings with feelings or personal issues with a group of peers.
D. ___ Designing the set for a play, joining the chess team, or joining the math club.
E. ___ Joining a musical group such as a jazz band, a chorus, or a rap group.
F. ___ Working as a writer for the school newspaper or joining the debate team.
G. ___ Painting murals on the school's walls.

SOURCE: Reprinted with permission from *History Alive!* 1999. Palo Alto, CA: Teachers' Curriculum Institute.

5. What Would You Like to Do in the Future?

What would you most like to be when you get older?

A. ___ A counselor, social worker, or teacher
B. ___ A dancer, actor, builder, or athlete
C. ___ A psychologist or poet
D. ___ A scientist, computer programmer, or banker
E. ___ A singer, songwriter, or musician
F. ___ A lawyer, writer, or journalist
G. ___ A cartoonist, painter, or graphic artist

Scoring Your Multiple Intelligences: Assessment 2

Copy the rankings you recorded into the boxes below, then add up the rankings for each letter.

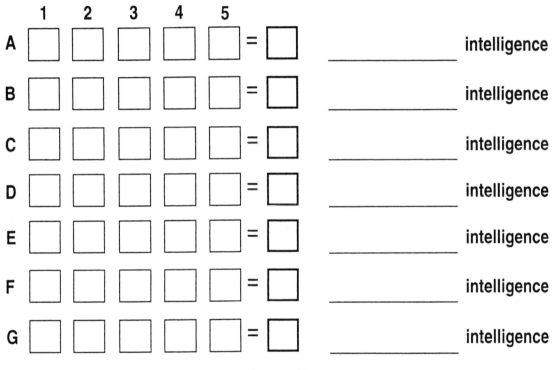

Teacher Answer Key

Note: Do not reveal these to students until after they have scored their tests.

A = interpersonal
B = bodily-kinesthetic
C = intrapersonal
D = logical-mathematical
E = musical-rhythmic
F = verbal-linguistic
G = visual-spatial

SOURCE: Reprinted with permission from *History Alive!* 1999. Palo Alto, CA: Teachers' Curriculum Institute.

CHECKLIST FOR ASSESSING STUDENTS' MULTIPLE INTELLIGENCES

Name of Student: _____

Check items that apply:

Linguistic Intelligence
_____ writes better than average for age
_____ spins tall tales or tells jokes and stories
_____ has a good memory for names, places, dates, or trivia
_____ enjoys word games
_____ enjoys reading books
_____ spells words accurately (or if preschool, does developmental spelling that is advanced for age)
_____ appreciates nonsense rhymes, puns, tongue twisters
_____ enjoys listening to the spoken word (stories, commentary on the radio, talking books)
_____ has a good vocabulary for age
_____ communicates to others in a highly verbal way

Other Linguistic Abilities:

Logical-Mathematical Intelligence
_____ asks a lot of questions about how things work
_____ enjoys working or playing with numbers
_____ enjoys math class (or if preschool, enjoys counting and doing other things with numbers)
_____ finds math and computer games interesting (or if no exposure to computers, enjoys other math or science games)
_____ enjoys playing chess, checkers, or other strategy games
_____ enjoys working on logic puzzles or brainteasers (or if preschool, enjoys hearing logical nonsense)
_____ enjoys putting things in categories, hierarchies, or other logical patterns
_____ likes to do experiments in science class or in free play
_____ shows interest in science-related subjects
_____ does well on Piagetian-type assessments of logical thinking

Other Logical-Mathematical Abilities:

SOURCE: Reprinted with permission from Armstrong, T. 2000. *Multiple intelligences in the classroom* (2nd ed.). Alexandria, VA: Association for Supervision and Curriculum Development.

CHECKLIST FOR ASSESSING STUDENTS' MULTIPLE INTELLIGENCES

Spatial Intelligence
_____ reports clear visual images
_____ reads maps, charts, and diagrams more easily than text (or if preschool, enjoys looking at more than text)
_____ daydreams a lot
_____ enjoys art activities
_____ good at drawings
_____ likes to view movies, slides, or other visual presentations
_____ enjoys doing puzzles, mazes, or similar visual activities
_____ builds interesting three-dimensional constructions (e.g., LEGO buildings)
_____ gets more out of pictures than words while reading
_____ doodles on workbooks, worksheets, or other materials

Other Spatial Abilities:

Bodily-Kinesthetic Intelligence
_____ excels in one or more sports (or if preschool, shows physical prowess advanced for age)
_____ moves, twitches, taps, or fidgets while seated for a long time in one spot
_____ cleverly mimics other people's gestures or mannerisms
_____ loves to take things apart and put them back together again
_____ puts his/her hands all over something he/she's just seen
_____ enjoys running, jumping, wrestling, or similar activities (or if older, will show these interests in a more "restrained" way—e.g., running to class, jumping over a chair)
_____ shows skill in a craft (e.g., woodworking, sewing, mechanics) or good fine-motor coordination in other ways
_____ has a dramatic way of expressing herself/himself
_____ reports different physical sensations while thinking or working
_____ enjoys working with clay or other tactile experiences (e.g., fingerpainting)

Other Bodily-Kinesthetic Abilities:

SOURCE: Reprinted with permission from Armstrong, T. 2000. _Multiple intelligences in the classroom_ (2nd ed.). Alexandria, VA: Association for Supervision and Curriculum Development.

CHECKLIST FOR ASSESSING STUDENTS' MULTIPLE INTELLIGENCES

Musical Intelligence

_____ tells you when music sounds off-key or disturbing in some other way

_____ remembers melodies of songs

_____ has a good singing voice

_____ plays a musical instrument or sings in a choir or other group (or if preschool, enjoys playing percussion instruments and/or singing in a group)

_____ has a rhythmic way of speaking and/or moving

_____ unconsciously hums to himself/herself

_____ taps rhythmically on the table or desk as he/she works

_____ sensitive to environmental noises (e.g., rain on the roof)

_____ responds favorably when a piece of music is put on

_____ sings songs that he/she has learned outside of the classroom

Other Musical Abilities:

Interpersonal Intelligence

_____ enjoys socializing with peers

_____ seems to be a natural leader

_____ gives advice to friends who have problems

_____ seems to be street-smart

_____ belongs to clubs, committees, organizations, or informal peer groups

_____ enjoys informally teaching other kids

_____ likes to play games with other kids

_____ has two or more close friends

_____ has a good sense of empathy or concern for others

_____ others seek out his/her company

Other Interpersonal Abilities:

SOURCE: Reprinted with permission from Armstrong, T. 2000. *Multiple intelligences in the classroom* (2nd ed.). Alexandria, VA: Association for Supervision and Curriculum Development.

CHECKLIST FOR ASSESSING STUDENTS' MULTIPLE INTELLIGENCES

Intrapersonal Intelligence

_____ displays a sense of independence or a strong will
_____ has a realistic sense of his/her abilities and weaknesses
_____ does well when left alone to play or study
_____ marches to the beat of a different drummer in his/her style of living and learning
_____ has an interest or hobby that he/she doesn't talk much about
_____ has a good sense of self-direction
_____ prefers working alone to working with others
_____ accurately expresses how he/she is feeling
_____ is able to learn from his/her failures and successes in life
_____ has good self-esteem

Other Intrapersonal Abilities:

Naturalist Intelligence

_____ talks a lot about favorite pets, or preferred spots in nature, during class sharing
_____ likes field trips in nature, to the zoo, or to a natural history museum
_____ shows sensitivity to natural formations (e.g., while walking outside with the class, will notice mountains, clouds; or if in an urban environment, may show this ability in sensitivity to popular culture "formations" such as sneakers or automobile styles)
_____ likes to water and tend to the plants in the classroom
_____ likes to hang around the gerbil cage, the aquarium, or the terrarium in class
_____ gets excited when studying about ecology, nature, plants, or animals
_____ speaks out in class for the rights of animals, or the preservation of planet earth
_____ enjoys doing nature projects, such as bird watching, butterfly or insect collections, tree study, or raising animals
_____ brings to school bugs, flowers, leaves, or other natural things to share with classmates or teachers
_____ does well in topics at school that involve living systems (e.g., biological topics in science, environmental issues in social studies)

Other Naturalist Abilities:

SOURCE: Reprinted with permission from Armstrong, T. 2000. *Multiple intelligences in the classroom* (2nd ed.). Alexandria, VA: Association for Supervision and Curriculum Development.

Resource C

An Example of an Internet Acceptable Use Policy Contract

Figure C.1 Internet Acceptable Use Policy—Pacoima Middle School, Los Angeles Unified School District

Student Name _____ (Please print)

PACOIMA MIDDLE SCHOOL ACCEPTABLE USE POLICY FOR COMPUTER NETWORKS

Your child has requested access to the Pacoima Middle School computer network. This access includes connections to computers through the Internet, which would connect your child with educational resources all over the world.

Please read Pacoima's Use Policy with your child. In accepting an account, your child accepts the responsibility of using the network in an appropriate manner. It is important that you understand his/her responsibilities as well. Your signature indicating that you have read and agreed to our Use Policy is necessary before an account will be issued.

I have read the Student Use Policy for Network Access at Pacoima Middle School and agree to use the school network in an appropriate manner.

_____   _____

Student Signature   Date

I have read the Student Use Policy for Network Access at Pacoima Middle School and give the school permission to issue an account to my child.

_____   _____

Parent Signature   Date

Figure C.2 Internet Acceptable Use Policy—Pacoima Middle School, Los Angeles Unified School District

STUDENT USE POLICY FOR NETWORK ACCESS AT PACOIMA MIDDLE SCHOOL

Introduction/Explanation of Purpose

On the school network and on the Internet, students and staff may participate in activities that support learning and teaching. With access to other networks and people around the world, you might have access to information that may not be appropriate. Pacoima Middle School has taken measures to prevent access to inappropriate information; however, we cannot control all the information available on the Internet. The school is not responsible for other people's actions or the quality and content of information available. We trust our students and staff to know what is appropriate and inappropriate. The following guidelines are intended to help you use the network appropriately. If a student does not follow our use policies listed here, his/her privilege of using the network may be withdrawn.

Use Policy

At all times, the Pacoima Standards must be followed: Is it safe? Is it kind? Is it appropriate?

- If you find yourself on an inappropriate site, it is your responsibility to **IMMEDIATELY** press the *back* button on the menu bar.

- At all times, your actions must take into account the rights of others.

- Respect the privacy of other network users.

- Do not use bad language, and do not send messages that violate the law or would be offensive to another person.

- Any use of Pacoima's network shall be for the exchange of information in order to help a person's education and research.

- Use your own software. It is against the law to copy other people's software. ONLY copy shareware, freeware, or software marked public domain.

- Do not spread computer viruses.

- Change your password frequently.

- Users of Pacoima's systems shall avoid congestion of the networks and interference with the work of other network users.

• Do not damage any networks or any equipment or system forming part of a network. Do not break or misuse anything in the computer room.

• Most of the Internet cannot be used to advertise or make money. Advertise only in appropriate areas of the Internet.

• NEVER give out personal information such as your home address or telephone number. Use the school's address instead, but not the school's phone number.

• Be familiar with these rules and how to use the Internet before getting online. If you have any questions about these rules, please ask your teacher so you can understand.

A Cooperative Work Group Lesson Plan Form

Subject Area

Title

GRADE RANGE

Objectives

At the end of this unit the students will:

- Understand

- Analyze

- Synthesize

- Evaluate

Materials

Internet Sites to Use Throughout the Unit

Title

URL
Description

Title

URL
Description

Title

URL
Description

Title

URL
Description

Title

URL
Description

Title

URL
Description

Title

URL
Description

Title

URL
Description

Title

URL
Description

Method

1.

2.

3.

4.

5.

6.

7.

8.

Assessment Suggestions

Use of the Multiple Intelligences

Intelligence	How it is addressed in the unit
Verbal-linguistic	
Logical-mathematical	
Visual-spatial	
Bodily-kinesthetic	
Musical	
Interpersonal	
Intrapersonal	
Naturalist	

Special Teacher Notes

References

Armstrong, T. (2000). *Multiple intelligences in the classroom* (2nd ed.). Alexandria, VA: Association for Supervision and Curriculum Development.

Barker, R. T., Gilbreath, G. H., & Stone, W. S. (1998). The interdisciplinary needs of organizations. Are new employees adequately equipped? *Journal of Management Development, 17*(3), 219–232.

Beebe, S. A., & Masterson, J. T. (1999). *Communicating in small groups: Principles and practices* (6th ed.). Glenview, IL: Scott, Foresman.

Bloom, B. S. (Ed.). (1953). *Taxonomy of educational objectives: Handbook I. Cognitive domain.* New York: David McKay.

Carnevale, A. P. (1991). *America and the new economy.* Research report. (ERIC Document Reproduction Service Number CE058361)

Carnevale, A. P. (1996). Liberal education and the new economy. *Liberal Education, 82*(2), 4–11.

Carnevale, A. P. (2002). Preparing for the future. *American School Board Journal, 189*(7), 26–29, 47.

Carnevale, A. P., Gainer, L. J., & Meltzer, A. S. (1990). *Workplace basics: The essential skills employers want.* San Francisco: Jossey-Bass.

Carnevale, A. P., & Porro, J. D. (1994). *Quality education: School reform for the new American economy.* Position paper. (ERIC Document Reproduction Service Number CE065765)

Caverly, D. C., Peterson, C., & Mandeville, T. (1997). A general model for professional development. *Educational Leadership, 55*(3) 56–59.

Checkley, K. (1997). The first seven . . . and the eighth. *Educational Leadership, 55*(1) 8–13.

Dede, C. (1997). Rethinking how to invest in technology. *Educational Leadership, 55*(3), 12–16.

Dewey, J. (1933). *How we think.* Chicago: Henry Regenery.

Dewey, J. (1959). The child and the curriculum. In M. Dworkin (Ed.), *Dewey on education.* New York: Columbia University, Teachers College, Bureau of Publications.

Dreir, H. S., Dawson, K. M., & Garofalo, J. (1997). Not your typical math class. *Educational Leadership, 55*(1), 8–13.

Eisner, E. W. (1994). *The educational imagination.* (3rd ed.). New York: Macmillan.

Fenstermacher, G. D. (1985). Time as the terminus of teaching: A philosophical perspective. In C. W. Fisher & D. C. Berliner (Eds.), *Perspectives on instructional time* (pp. 97–108). New York: Longman.

Filipovic, Z. (1994). *Zlata's diary: A child's life in Sarajevo* (C. Pribichevich-Zoric, Trans.). New York: Viking Penguin.

Gardner, H. (1993). *Multiple intelligences: The theory in practice.* New York: Basic Books.

Gardner, H. (1999). *Intelligence reframed: Multiple intelligences for the 21st century.* New York: Basic Books.

Glister, P. (1997). A new digital literacy: A conversation with Paul Glister. *Educational Leadership, 55*(3), 6–11.

Hackman, J. R. (2002). *Leading teams: Setting the stage for great performances.* Boston: Harvard Business School Press.

Hackman, J. R., Lawler, E. E., III, & Porter, L. W. (1983). *Perspectives on behavior in organizations.* New York: McGraw-Hill.

Hare, A. P. (1976). *Handbook of small group research.* New York: Free Press.

Harnischfeger, A. & Wiley, D. C. (1976). The teaching-learning process in elementary schools: A synoptic view. *Curriculum Inquiry, 6,* 5–43.

Harnischfeger, A., & Wiley, D. C. (1985). Origins of active learning time. In C. W. Fisher & D. C. Berlinger (Eds.), *Perspectives on instructional time* (pp. 133–156). New York: Longman.

Henerson, M. E., Morris, L. L., & Fitz-Gibbon, C. T. (1978). *How to measure attitudes.* Beverly Hills, CA: Sage.

History Alive! (1999). Palo Alto, CA: Teachers' Curriculum Institute.

Jacobs, G. M., & James, J. E. (1994, March). *A comparison of workplace groups with groups in education.* Paper presented at the Annual Meeting of Teachers of English to Speakers of Other Languages, Baltimore, MD. (ERIC Document Reproduction Service Number ED369922)

Johnson, D. W., & Johnson, R. T. (1986). *Learning together and alone* (2nd ed.). Englewood Cliffs, NJ: Prentice Hall.

Johnson, D. W., & Johnson, R. T. (1999). *What makes cooperative learning work?* Tokyo: JALT Applied Materials.

Joyce, B. (1985). Models for teaching thinking. *Educational Leadership, 42*(8), 4–7.

Joyce, B., & Calhoun, E. (1996). *Creating learning experiences: The role of instructional theory and research.* Alexandria, VA: Association for Supervision and Curriculum Development.

Joyce, B., & Calhoun, E. (1998). *Learning to teach inductively.* Boston: Allyn and Bacon.

Joyce, B., Calhoun, E., & Hopkins, D. (2002). *Models of learning: Tools for teaching* (2nd ed.). Buckingham, England: Open University Press.

Joyce, B., Showers, B., & Rolheiser-Bennett, C. (1987). Staff development and student learning: A synthesis of research on models of teaching. *Educational Leadership, 45*(2), 11–23.

Joyce, B., & Weil, M. (2000). *Models of teaching* (6th ed.). Boston: Allyn and Bacon.

Kagan, S. (1989). The structural approach to cooperative learning. *Educational Leadership, 47*(4), 12–15.

Klein, P. D. (1997). Multiplying the problems of intelligence by eight: A critique of Gardner's theory. *Canadian Journal of Education, 22*(4), 377–394.

Kozlowski, S. (1995). Organizational change, informal learning, and adaptation: Emerging trends in training and continuing education. *Journal of Continuing Higher Education, 43*(1), 2–11.

Latham, A. (1999). Computers and achievement. *Educational Leadership, 56*(5), 87–88.

Maclachlan, P. (1985). *Sarah, plain and tall.* New York: Harper and Row.

Mandel, S. (1991). *Responses to cooperative learning processes among elementary-age students.* (ERIC Document Reproduction Service Number ED 332808)

Mandel, S. (1998). *Social studies in the cyberage: Applications with cooperative learning.* Arlington Heights, IL: Skylight Training and Publishing.

Mandel, S. (1999). *Virtual field trips in the cyberage: A content mapping approach.* Arlington Heights, IL: Skylight Professional Development.

Menken, A., & Schwartz, S. (1996). "God help the outcasts." On *The Hunchback of Notre Dame* [CD]. Burbank, CA: Walt Disney Records.

Nelson, R., & Watras, J. (1981). The scientific movement: American education and the emergence of the technological society. *Journal of Thought, 16*(1), 49–71.

Scieszka, J. (1995). *Math curse.* New York: Viking Children's Books.

Sharan, S. (1994). *Handbook of cooperative learning methods.* Westport, CT: Greenwood.

Sharan, S., Kussel, P., Hertz-Lazarowitz, R., Bejarano, Y., Raviv, S., & Sharan, Y. (1984). *Cooperative learning in the classroom: Research in desegregated schools.* Hillsdale, NJ: Lawrence Erlbaum.

Sharan, S., Shachar, H., & Levine, T. (1999). *The innovative school: Organization and instruction.* Westport, CT: Bergin and Garvey.

Sharan, Y., & Sharan, S. (1992). *Expanding cooperative learning through group investigation.* New York: Teachers College Press.

Slavin, R. E. (1995). *Cooperative learning: Theory, research, and practice* (2nd ed.). Englewood Cliffs, NJ: Prentice Hall.

Slavin, R. E., Madden, N. A., & Stevens, R. J. (1989). Cooperative learning models for the 3 R's. *Educational Leadership, 47*(4), 22–28.

Thelen, H. A. (1954). *Dynamics of groups at work.* Chicago: University of Chicago Press.

Thelen, H. A. (1960). *Education and the human quest.* New York: Harper and Row.

Tyler, R. W. (1949). *Basic principles of curriculum and instruction.* Chicago: University of Chicago Press.

Wayne, F. S., and others. (1992). Vital communication skills and competencies in the workforce of the 1990s. *Journal of Education for Business, 67*(3), 141–146.

Index

**CORWIN
PRESS**

The Corwin Press logo—a raven striding across an open book—represents the happy union of courage and learning. We are a professional-level publisher of books and journals for K-12 educators, and we are committed to creating and providing resources that embody these qualities. Corwin's motto is "Success for All Learners."